CANADA'S
OLYMPIC DIARY

CANADA'S
OLYMPIC DIARY

A Day-by-Day Account of the 2010 Winter Games

THE CANADIAN PRESS

KEY PORTER BOOKS

Library and Archives Canada Cataloguing in Publication

Canada's Olympic diary : a day by day account of the 2010 winter games / the Canadian Press.

ISBN 978-1-55470-337-1

1. Winter Olympic Games (21st : 2010 : Vancouver, B.C.).
I. Canadian Press

GV722.2010C36 2010   796.98   C2010-900818-9

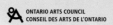

The publisher gratefully acknowledges the support of the Canada Council for the Arts and the Ontario Arts Council for its publishing program. We acknowledge the support of the Government of Ontario through the Ontario Media Development Corporation's Ontario Book Initiative.

We acknowledge the financial support of the Government of Canada through the Book Publishing Industry Development Program (BPIDP) for our publishing activities.

Key Porter Books Limited
Six Adelaide Street East, Tenth Floor
Toronto, Ontario
Canada M5C 1H6

www.keyporter.com

Photo Editor: Graeme Roy, The Canadian Press
Text Editor: Patti Tasko, The Canadian Press
Project Editor: Lloyd Davis, Butterfield 8 Inc.
Design: First Image

Printed and bound in Canada
10 11 12 13 14 6 5 4 3 2 1

THE CANADIAN PRESS

High-quality prints of many of the photographs in this book may be purchased for personal use.

For information about acquiring images from The Canadian Press, please visit us at: www.cpimages.com and www.thecanadianpress.com CALL 1-866-599-0599 or email us at archives@cpimages.com

Contents

Prague, 2003

The story begins

BY JIM MORRIS

WHEN IOC President Jacques Rogge announced on July 2, 2003, in Prague that Vancouver had been awarded the 2010 Winter Olympics, it marked a crossroads in the Games' journey to Canada.

One long stretch filled with potholes and surprises had ended. Another, with twists, anxiety and the promise of triumph, beckoned.

Rogge's announcement followed a day of nail-biting tension. Vancouver's Olympic dream had almost turned into a nightmare when Pyeongchang in South Korea received 51 votes on the first ballot, falling just three votes short of the 54 needed to win. Vancouver trailed badly with 40 while Salzburg, Austria, was eliminated with just 16.

On the second and deciding ballot, Vancouver edged Pyeongchang 56-53.

"I was scared," John Furlong, head of the Vancouver bid, admitted at the time. Furlong would later be named chief executive officer of the Vancouver 2010 Winter Games Organizing Committee.

Vancouver was the first city to make a scheduled 45-minute presentation to the 113 members of the International Olympic Committee gathered in the Czech city.

The 100 Vancouver delegates, including 11 members of the presentation team, were led into the conference hall at the Hilton Hotel by two Mounties. Every delegate carried a $1 coin in their pocket for luck.

Prime Minister Jean Chrétien, bid committee chairman Jack Poole, Furlong, hockey great Wayne Gretzky and Catriona le May Doan, a two-time Olympic gold medallist in speedskating, addressed the IOC.

The $275,000 presentation included a video, complete with a soundtrack performed by Vancouver native Bryan Adams.

The video showed green forests and big city buildings, skiers on the slopes at Whistler and kayaks on English Bay. There were smiling Mounties and children doing ballet.

While confident with their presentation, the Canadians were still worried. The Koreans had spent the previous several days lobbying hard. Even before voting had ended, one Korean website proclaimed Pyeongchang the winner.

In Prague on July 2, 2003, hockey star Wayne Gretzky, Prime Minister Jean Chrétien and former Canadian Olympic speedskater Catriona le May Doan celebrate the awarding of the Games to Vancouver.

(Jonathan Hayward/The Canadian Press)

The Canadian delegation listens as John Furlong presents Vancouver's Olympic bid to IOC members in Prague.
(Jonathan Hayward/ The Canadian Press)

A supporter watches the giant screen at GM Place in Vancouver, waiting to hear if the city's bid is successful.
(Chuck Stoody/The Canadian Press)

Canadians gathered at GM Place celebrate the news of Vancouver's win on July 2, 2003.

(Chuck Stoody/The Canadian Press)

When Rogge finally began to announce the winning city, he hesitated. Senator Nancy Greene Raine, Canada's skiing star from the 1968 Winter Games, later said she was afraid Pyeongchang had won and Rogge was having trouble pronouncing the city's name.

She need not have worried. The Games were coming to Vancouver.

The moment Rogge announced Vancouver's victory, Canadians jammed into the sweltering hot hotel lobby started singing "O Canada" and waving Maple Leafs.

A huge crowd watching at GM Place in Vancouver greeted the verdict with frenzied cheering. A giant, impromptu conga line danced through Whistler Village.

Bidding for the Games cost $35 million. Vancouver painted itself as a sophisticated urban centre on the shore of the Pacific Ocean with a world-class alpine resort at Whistler, just 120 kilometres north.

"Obviously the best bid won," said Rogge later.

Awarding the Games to Vancouver resulted in several firsts.

It was the first time a Winter Olympics had been held at sea level. Vancouver was the largest city ever invited to host the Winter Games and, with an average February temperature of 4.8 degrees Celsius, the warmest.

Opening and closing ceremonies were held at B.C. Place Stadium, the first time in Winter Olympic history those events took place indoors.

Vancouver's road to the Games began in 1998, when the city was chosen as Canada's candidate to bid for the 2010 Games, beating out Calgary and Quebec City in a two-stage vote by the Canadian Olympic Committee. In the first round of balloting on Nov. 21, Vancouver collected 26 votes, Quebec City 25 and Calgary 21. In a final run-off held on Dec. 3, Vancouver had 40 votes against 32 for Quebec City.

Internationally, Vancouver was one of eight cities bidding for the Games. Also in the running were Andorra la Vella, Andorra; Bern, Switzerland; Harbin, China; Jaca, Spain; Sarajevo, Bosnia-Herzegovina; Pyeongchang and Salzburg.

Jennifer Goepel (right) shows her joy at the news the Olympics are headed for Vancouver.
(Richard Lam/The Canadian Press)

Larry Grant, councillor of the Musqueam band (left), and Chief Ian Campbell of the Squamish Nation, on the drum, at GM Place on July 2, 2003.

(Chuck Stoody/The Canadian Press)

In August 2002, the IOC shortened the list to Bern, Pyeongchang, Salzburg and Vancouver.

In September 2002, voters in Bern scuttled that city's Olympic bid. They rejected a call by organizers for cash to help pay for the Games. Anti-Games advocates in Vancouver took note and quickly began pressing for a referendum in their city.

When Larry Campbell was elected the city's mayor in 2002, one of his promises was to hold a plebiscite on Vancouver hosting the Games. Even though the plebiscite was non-binding, Rogge said the Games would not go to a city where there's "overwhelming negative sentiment."

Vancouver's Yes side, which supported the Games bid, ran a splashy campaign. It spent over $700,000 on rallies, newspaper ads and life-size posters wrapped around buildings.

If the Yes side was Broadway, the No group was community theatre. It operated on a budget of under $5,000 and relied heavily on anger toward the policies of the provincial Liberal government.

The vote was held Feb. 22, 2003. Almost half of the city's 293,000 eligible voters turned out, with the Yes side taking 64 per cent of the ballots. The IOC said the result "looks strong."

Members of the Vancouver bid committee breathed a sigh of relief but had little time to celebrate. An IOC evaluation team was coming to tour the area, visit proposed venues and write a detailed analysis of all the components of Vancouver's bid.

Gerhard Heiberg, the evaluation team's head, appeared to deliver Vancouver's hopes a blow during a visit to Whistler. "One problem only: it's too far from Vancouver," Heiberg said.

The comment made headlines in the city's newspapers and international news. Heiberg tried to make amends later by saying if Vancouver was awarded the Games, "you are going to show the world perhaps the best Winter Olympics ever." B.C.'s provincial government promised to improve the highway between Vancouver and Whistler as part of the Games proposal.

When the evaluation commission released its final report, Vancouver's bid received high marks. The environmental plans were called "professional and ambitious," the budget "fundamentally sound" and bid leaders were praised for a "thorough and detailed plan based on risk minimization."

Heading into the vote at Prague, most experts considered Vancouver the frontrunner among the three cities. Privately, Furlong expressed concern that Pyeongchang could pull off an upset.

Cheering crowds awaited the successful bid committee upon its return to Canada. With the Games finally coming to Vancouver, the real work was about to begin.

The Vancouver organizing committee, known locally as VANOC, was created with Poole being named chairman of the 20-member board of directors. A seven-member search committee chose Furlong as the chief executive officer.

Sadly, Poole never saw his Olympic vision turn into reality.

He died in October after a lengthy battle with pancreatic cancer. His death came on the day after the flame for the Vancouver Games was lit in Olympia, Greece.

Jack Poole, chief of the Vancouver bid, in Prague.

(Jonathan Hayward/The Canadian Press)

The torch run

45,000 kilometres, 1,000 communities, 12,000 pairs of mitts

BY STEPHANIE LEVITZ

OLYMPIC ORGANIZERS conceived of a relay that would tell the story of Canada, a torch held aloft by one set of red mittens at a time, passed through 12,000 pairs.

They didn't expect those mittens to end up everywhere — from the fins of Huskie the Muskie, the giant fish that welcomes visitors to Kenora, Ont., to the giant claws of the T. Rex that looms over the downtown of Drumheller, Alta.

The torch, perhaps the most poignant symbol of the Olympics, was lit using the sun's rays and a mirror in an elaborate, theatrical ceremony at the site of the ancient Olympics on Oct. 22, 2009. It was carried for a week through Greece before being carefully loaded onto a Canadian Forces military plane and flown to Canada.

It touched down in Victoria on Oct. 30, 2009, and set off on the longest domestic relay in the history of the Games.

Over 106 days, the torch covered some 45,000 kilometres, visiting 1,000 communities. "This is for all of Canada," said speedskater Catriona le May Doan, a four-time Olympian who, along with triathlete Simon Whitfield, was the first to carry the torch.

Day One provided an inkling of what was to come.

Thousands of people packed the grounds of the B.C. legislature to watch the arrival of the flame, a scene repeated itself over and over again.

The protests were also there on Day One. The flame relay had been used to great effect to highlight China's treatment of Tibet before the Beijing Summer Games in 2008. Canadian agitators said they'd do the same to draw attention to Canadian injustices such as poverty and unresolved aboriginal land claims.

That first evening, an anti-Olympic protest turned unruly, forcing torch run organizers and police to divert the relay, dampening the excitement of a handful of torchbearers who, rather than running their 300-metre stretch, instead stood on the side of a road and handed the flame off to one another.

Ruth Sadler (left) passes Raph Bruhwiler
the torch as he surfs by on Long Beach
near Tofino, B.C., on Nov. 1, 2009.

(Jonathan Hayward/The Canadian Press)

Beth Idlout-Kheraj, 15, carries the Olympic flame, protected in a miner's lantern from high winds and -40 C temperatures, in Resolute Bay, Nunavut, on Nov. 9, 2009. (Jonathan Hayward/The Canadian Press)

Viking impersonators watch Frank Humber carry the flame into a Viking hut in L'Anse aux Meadows, N.L., on Nov. 12, 2009. (Jonathan Hayward/The Canadian Press)

Michael Dinn carries the Olympic flame in a traditional fishing dory in Petty Harbour, N.L., on Nov. 13, 2009.

(Jonathan Hayward/The Canadian Press)

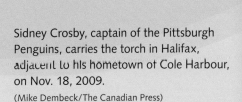

Sidney Crosby, captain of the Pittsburgh Penguins, carries the torch in Halifax, adjacent to his hometown of Cole Harbour, on Nov. 18, 2009.

(Mike Dembeck/The Canadian Press)

Lance Berrisford (left) passes the flame to Brian Petts in Point Pelee National Park on the shores of Lake Erie, the southernmost point of the Canadian mainland, on Dec. 23, 2009.

(Dave Chidley/The Canadian Press)

Weeks later, in Kahnawake, Que., a last-minute negotiation saw the relay cancelled in favour of a simpler event to avoid inflaming Mohawk-RCMP tensions.

While the flame passed within an hour's drive of 90 per cent of the country's population, it also ended up in places most Canadians never see. In Alert, the northernmost inhabited point in the world, 20 members of Canadian Forces Station Alert who dubbed themselves the "Frozen Chosen" ran with the torch.

It visited L'Anse aux Meadows, an archeological site believed to be the place where the Vikings had a settlement a millennium ago.

There were countless heartwarming moments along the route, including three marriage proposals.

There were also the frustrating ones. In Churchill, Man., the famed polar bears couldn't be found when it was time for a photograph with the flame.

The flame also went out a couple of times in the north, forcing torch run officials to make an on-the-fly adjustment to keep it going in extremely high winds.

Torchbearers snowmobiled, jogged, surfed and skied with the flame, and even those used to the limelight gasped

Vicky Sunohara, a member of Canada's Olympic hockey team in 1998, 2002 and 2006, carries the torch at Nathan Phillips Square in Toronto on Dec. 17, 2009.

(Darren Calabrese/The Canadian Press)

Singer Shania Twain lights the Olympic cauldron with the Olympic flame at Hollinger Park in her hometown of Timmins, Ont., on Jan. 1, 2010.

(Pawel Dwulit/The Canadian Press)

Richard Hardy carries the flame in a long house in Comox, B.C., on Nov. 2, 2009.

(Jonathan Hayward/The Canadian Press)

out descriptions of wonder after their 300 metres of holding the torch aloft.

"You look at the people out there, you see the signs of the excitement," said hockey star Sidney Crosby about the massive crush of fans who slowed his jog in Halifax to a crawl. "You never dream of carrying the torch. For me, that wasn't something that I ever thought would be a possibility."

International media also paid attention. The Canadian Tourism Commission brought 14 athletes and broadcasters from key markets like India and China to run with the torch. In addition to their run, the celebrities participated in local activities like dogsledding, wine tours and hockey games.

Suddenly, footage of Saskatchewan was playing in Paris.

The cross-country relay's final day played out in a collection of interconnected scenes in Vancouver, woven together by the dozens of torchbearers carrying the flame home, thousands of spectators lining the streets, and some protesters whose anti-Olympic chants mixed with the sounds of cowbells, noisemakers and bagpipes.

There were even brushes with Hollywood fame as the Terminator himself, California Gov. Arnold Schwarzenegger, picked up the torch.

The relay's official end point in Vancouver was an aboriginal pavilion staged by the Four Host First Nations, a collection of aboriginal bands. The flame was used to light a small cauldron on stage, marking the last time the flame was on public display until the final torchbearer ignited the cauldron at the opening ceremonies.

Aboard a dragon boat on Vancouver's False Creek, Hugh Fisher of Pemberton, B.C., carries the Olympic torch on Feb. 12, 2010, the final day of the flame's cross-Canada journey.

(Darryl Dyck/The Canadian Press)

PERFORMANCE ANXIETY?

Lighting of the Olympic flame, the marquee moment of the opening ceremonies, was briefly delayed as one of four pillars designed to emerge from the floor of B.C. Place to support the central cauldron malfunctioned.

HUGHES STANDS OUT

In a departure from the rest of her teammates, Canadian flag-bearer Clara Hughes wore a distinctive tuque, a gift from the Four Host First Nations, into B.C. Place for the opening ceremonies.

Wearing black armbands, members of the Georgian team proceed solemnly into B.C. Place at the opening ceremonies. Earlier in the day, Georgian luger Nodar Kumaritashvili died during a training run.

(Jonathan Hayward/The Canadian Press)

Tragedy amidst celebration

BY JAMES McCARTEN

IN THE end, it began with The Great One.

It was hockey icon Wayne Gretzky — with a little help from friends Rick Hansen, Steve Nash, Nancy Greene Raine and Catriona le May Doan — who ferried the Olympic flame to its lofty perch in downtown Vancouver.

But neither the Stanley Cup legend, the flame's arrival after an epic 106-day, 45,000-kilometre journey, or the start in earnest — finally — of the most anticipated Canadian sports event since the 1988 Games could cushion the blow of an unspeakable tragedy.

Just hours before the cauldron was lit, Georgian luger Nodar Kumaritashvili, 21, was killed when he lost control of his sled on the fearsome ice track in Whistler, B.C., hurtling out of the icy pipeline and slamming into a concrete pillar.

"You compete with such bravery, conviction and pride at these Games," Vancouver organizing committee president John Furlong, considered the event's Canadian custodian, told athletes from the 82 nations taking part.

"You now have the added burden to shine and be united around your fallen colleague Nodar. May you carry his Olympic dream on your shoulders and compete with his spirit in your hearts."

Nonetheless, the most dramatic moments of the opening ceremonies were as bold as the goals Vancouver organizers had set for their Games — changing not only the way the world thinks about Canada, but how Canada thinks of itself.

The technology-heavy show, meant to capture the Canadian spirit, began with the dramatic entry of a snowboarder who soared through giant Olympic rings and ended in heart-stopping panic when the Olympic cauldron briefly refused to rise from the floor.

But what was meant to be a celebration before the true work of the Olympics had already been tempered by loss.

When Kumaritashvili's seven crestfallen teammates entered B.C. Place stadium, they were clad in black scarves and hats, and some of them managed weak waves to the crowd of 60,600 people. Every one of them was on their feet in tribute.

"It's a terrible tragedy, and I think that that's (the) humanity of the Games," said women's hockey captain Hayley Wickenheiser.

"Why did it have to happen to him? Why at the Olympics? We all kind of wonder that."

The show, of course, went on.

Gov. Gen. Michaëlle Jean waved and danced along with the crowd as the Canadian team made their grand entrance, led by Clara Hughes, the 1,000-watt speedskater with the flaming red mane.

"I feel like the most beautiful maple leaf has fallen into my hands and that's the Canadian flag," Hughes beamed before marching out into the blazing spotlight.

For the Canadians, the hard part, of course, was yet to come.

The only thing grander than the spectacle of opening night were the expectations that Canada would lead the medal count.

Before 2010, Canada had never won an Olympic gold medal on Canadian soil. On Day 1, it wasn't a question of if, but when, and by whom.

An RCMP guard of honour carries the Canadian flag into B.C. Place at the opening ceremonies on Feb. 12, 2010.
(Nathan Denette/The Canadian Press)

A snowboarder flies through the Olympic rings,
signalling the beginning of the opening ceremonies.

(Nathan Denette/The Canadian Press)

To symbolize the theme of the opening ceremonies, "Landscape of a Dream," a silhouetted performer walks across the floor of B.C. Place, transformed into a scene from the frozen North.
(Jonathan Hayward/The Canadian Press)

Aboriginal dancers representing the Four Host First Nations perform.
(Darryl Dyck/The Canadian Press)

Totem poles representing the Four Host First Nations extend their arms to welcome the athletes, dignitaries and spectators to the Olympic Winter Games in Vancouver.
(Ryan Remiorz/The Canadian Press)

Led by speedskater Clara Hughes, who had been chosen as flag-bearer, the Canadian team parades into B.C. Place.
(Robert Skinner/The Canadian Press)

Dancers and fiddlers, representing the Celtic-
influenced culture of Eastern Canada, surround
a stage decorated with red maple leaves.
(Jonathan Hayward/The Canadian Press)

Joined by skiers and snowboarders suspended in mid-air, performers dressed as speedskaters circle a mountain peak. During the opening ceremonies, images and special lighting effects were projected against any available surface.

(Nathan Denette/The Canadian Press)

Eight Canadian celebrities from various walks of life carry the Olympic flag into B.C. place. At left (front to back) are Betty Fox, mother of cancer activist Terry Fox; race-car driver Jacques Villeneuve; singer Anne Murray; and hockey player Bobby Orr. At right (front to back) are actor Donald Sutherland; figure skater Barbara Ann Scott-King, a gold medallist at the 1948 Games in St-Moritz; Sen. Roméo Dallaire; and astronaut Julie Payette.

(Jonathan Hayward/The Canadian Press)

Performers circle the flaming Olympic cauldron. The final four torch-bearers — Wayne Gretzky, who played on the men's hockey team at Nagano in 1998 and was executive director of Team Canada in 2002 at Salt Lake City and 2006 at Turin; Steve Nash, captain of the men's basketball team at Sydney in 2000; skier Nancy Greene Raine, an Olympic gold medallist at Grenoble in 1968; and speedskater Catriona le May Doan, a gold medallist at Nagano in 1998 and Salt Lake City in 2002 — had each been chosen to take part in the lighting ceremony. A mechanical glitch prevented one of the four pillars from rising into place, forcing le May Doan to look on while the others lit the flame. (Jonathan Hayward/The Canadian Press)

SKI JUMPING

Stefan Read, 22, of Edmonton, lands a jump during a qualifying round at Whistler Olympic Park. Individual normal hill ski jumping was the first event to be contested at the Vancouver Games. (Boris Minkevich/The Canadian Press)

Wayne Gretzky stands before a second, outdoor, cauldron after lighting it to conclude the opening ceremonies of the Winter Olympic Games. (Adrian Wyld/The Canadian Press)

DAY 2

NO, CANADA!

Stories on British Columbia's inclement weather, allegations that Canada violated Olympian ideals, and the social and financial costs of the Games to the province's underprivileged emerged in some international storylines. The warm, wet weather had the *New York Times*, for one, wondering whether the International Olympic Committee made a poor choice of venue.

TRACK TWEAK CRITIQUED

Canadian sliders had a hard time masking their disappointment at changes to the track they had been practising on for two years. Said luger Regan Lauscher of Red Deer, Alta.: "The finesse that you really need to feel on this track is changed when the speeds are different, so it's disappointing."

CAN'T GET NEXT TO YOU

Less than 24 hours after the lighting of the outdoor Olympic cauldron, awe turned to disappointment for thousands of spectators hoping to get a closer look, only to discover it had been encircled by a chain-link fence.

Rain clouds, silver lining

BY JAMES MCCARTEN

THE EXPRESSION on Jennifer Heil's face said it all.

Flanked by two jubilant U.S. skiers each brandishing the American flag, Heil's forced smile and dejected posture made it clear she was less than satisfied with silver — the first medal of any colour for Canada at the 2010 Winter Games.

The fresh-faced 26-year-old moguls skier from Spruce Grove, Alta., was unseated in Saturday's rain-soaked final by pigtailed U.S. rival Hannah Kearney, 24. Another American, 30-year-old Shannon Bahrke, took bronze.

Heil's aw-shucks attitude and trademark megawatt smile — she credited her performance to the support of Canadian fans from coast to coast — did little to mask her disappointment.

"I definitely felt like I could have done better, there's no doubt about it," she said afterward. "I was shooting for a gold tonight. But I really do feel like I won silver."

Vancouver Olympic organizers might have felt the same way.

First, there was the unco-operative weather. Then the tragic death of Georgian luger Nodar Kumaritashvili. On Friday, a technical snafu marred the opening ceremonies, which culminated in a lopsided-looking Olympic cauldron.

Saturday brought something even uglier.

Clearly spoiling for a fight, black-clad protesters equipped with ski goggles, vinegar-soaked face masks and other tear-gas countermeasures vented their anger on downtown Vancouver, smashing windows, splashing paint and clashing with police.

Tourists and locals alike were left shaking their heads.

"When you break things like this, you alienate regular people who might have agreed with your point of view," said 46-year-old Vancouver resident Isabella Mori.

"It feels like an attack on everyday people."

Aside from Heil's medal and a vicious 18-0 drubbing of Slovakia by the Canadian women's hockey team, there was little else on the first full day of competition to console Canadian fans.

Canada was shut out of the medals in the short-track speedskating men's 1,500 metres after favourite Charles Hamelin, 25, from Ste-Julie, Que., failed to advance out of the semifinals. Teammate Olivier Jean briefly set a new Olympic record of 2:14.279 in his heat, but fell in the semifinal. He still advanced after winning an interference appeal ending up fourth in the final.

In Whistler, the men's downhill — where Canada had pinned its medal hopes on Manuel Osborne-Paradis of

Invermere, B.C. — was rescheduled because of a slushy course, amplifying concerns about B.C.'s unfriendly weather.

The controversial luge track re-opened for training, with the men's starting point moved farther down the track and a new wooden barrier installed at the scene of Georgia's heartbreaking tragedy.

Some of the sliders, their spirits visibly dampened, sported black strips of tape on their helmets as they resumed their training. Kumaritashvili's fellow slider, Levan Gureshidze, opted to withdraw from the Games entirely.

The first gold of the 2010 Olympics went to Swiss ski jumper Simon Ammann, who snatched the prize from Polish veteran Adam Malysz with a thrilling leap in the final run of the day.

FREESTYLE SKIING SILVER

Jennifer Heil of Spruce Grove, Alta., catches air as she performs the last jump of her qualifying run at the women's freestyle moguls.

(Tara Walton/The Canadian Press)

SHORT-TRACK SPEEDSKATING

Marianne St-Gelais (centre) of St-Félicien, Que., prepares to pass British competitor Sarah Lindsay (left) in a women's 500-metre heat at the Pacific Coliseum. Tatiana Borodulina of Australia is at right.

(Paul Chiasson/The Canadian Press)

FREESTYLE SKIING   SILVER

Jennifer Heil celebrates her silver medal — Canada's first of the 2010 Games — at the flower ceremony after the women's freestyle moguls final.

(Tara Walton/The Canadian Press)

SHORT-TRACK SPEEDSKATING

Olivier Jean (left) of Montreal leads the pack during a men's 1,500-metre heat. The 25-year-old Jean, competing at his first Olympics, won the heat, then placed fourth in the final ranking.

(Robert Skinner/The Canadian Press)

BIATHLON

Zina Kocher drops to the ground after crossing the finish line in the women's 7.5-kilometre sprint in Whistler. The 27-year-old from Red Deer, Alta., placed 65th.

(Andrew Vaughan/The Canadian Press)

SPEEDSKATING

Lucas Makowsky of Regina skates in the final of the men's 5,000 metres at the Richmond Olympic Oval. Makowsky placed 13th in his Olympic debut.

(Rick Eglinton/The Canadian Press)

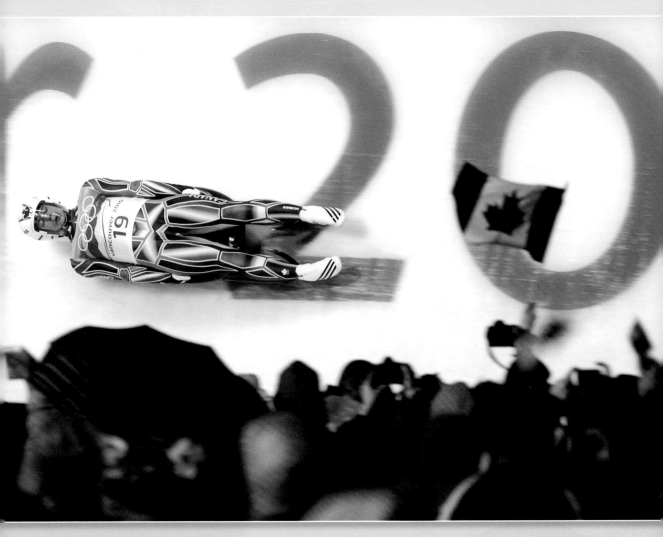

LUGE

Jeff Christie of Calgary competes during the first run of the men's singles at the Whistler Sliding Centre. (Jeff McIntosh/The Canadian Press)

HOCKEY

Caroline Ouellette (left) speaks with Slovakian goaltender Zuzana Tomcikova, who saved 49 of the 67 shots she faced, after Team Canada's 18-0 victory in their preliminary-round game at Canada Hockey Place. Ouellette, 30, from Montreal, scored a goal and assisted on four others. (Scott Gardner/The Canadian Press)

DAY 3

REFUNDS AT CYPRESS

Organizers were forced to shut down the general-admission section of the snowboarding venue at Cypress Mountain because of safety concerns caused by rain. Refunds of the $50 ticket price were to be paid to some 8,000 spectators.

THEY'RE NO FASHION SLACK-ERS

The pants worn by the Norwegian men's curling team at the Games seemed to come straight out of an Austin Powers movie. Featuring red, white and blue diamonds, the pants were made by Loudmouth Golf, the brand made famous by pro golfer John Daly. "It's just that it's Norwegian colours and our shirts weren't that bright, so we just figured we would spice it up a little bit with some colours," said Norwegian second Christoffer Svae.

PLUS DE FRANÇAIS, S'IL VOUS PLAÎT

Quebec Premier Jean Charest, federal Heritage Minister James Moore and Official Languages Commissioner Graham Fraser were among those who expressed disappointment at what they saw as a shortage of French-language content during the Games' opening ceremonies.

Golden moguls moment

BY JAMES MCCARTEN

FOR CANADA, it was a golden Games moment 34 years in the making — and it very nearly went Down Under courtesy of a Canadian-born Aussie.

Men's moguls skier Alexandre Bilodeau, 22, of Rosemère, Que., became an instant national hero on the second full day of competition when he stripped top-ranked rival Dale Begg-Smith, who competes for Australia despite having been born in Vancouver, of the first Olympic gold medal to be won on home soil by a Canadian.

Canada was denied gold both in Montreal in 1976 and again in Calgary in 1988, and another home Games without a gold would have dealt an Olympic-sized blow to the national psyche. "It's a dream realized," said Bilodeau, who also boldly predicted it would turn out to be just the first of many more. "It's just the beginning of the party."

Begg-Smith was in the catbird seat — in this case, the first-place position among the fluffy white beanbag chairs reserved for the top three in the standings — when Bilodeau came down the mountain, blistering the bumps and sailing coolly off the kickers.

Bilodeau punched the air with his fists and gave an ecstatic, frenzied crowd the thumbs-up as he ascended the podium. His Canadian-born rival could only manage a scowl.

Michael Chambers, president of the Canadian Olympic Committee, likened the moment to what's been called the most important goal in Canadian hockey history: Paul Henderson's winning marker in the 1972 Summit Series against the USSR.

"Where were you," he wondered rhetorically, "when Alex Bilodeau won the first gold medal on Canadian soil?"

Earlier in the day, Ottawa long-track speedskater Kristina Groves, 33, earned a warm bear hug from her fellow Canadian racer, the flame-haired flag-bearer Clara Hughes, after gutting out a bronze-medal finish in the women's 3,000 metres.

Czech Martina Sablikova claimed the gold and Stephanie Beckert of Germany the silver, while Hughes, from Glen Sutton, Que., was fifth in what was the second-to-last race of her career. Winnipeg's Cindy Klassen, a five-time medallist at the 2006 Turin Games, finished 14th.

"I got to watch my training partner, my teammate and my friend skate the 3,000-metre race of her life," Hughes gushed afterward. "It was a great day for our team."

Men's moguls competitors inspect the course prior to qualifying runs at Cypress Mountain.

(Darryl Dyck/The Canadian Press)

Though the persistent rain finally gave way to brilliant sunshine in Vancouver, such was not the case in Whistler. But rotten weather didn't keep 24-year-old Quebec City biathlete Jean-Philippe LeGuellec from a triumphant sixth-place finish in the men's biathlon 10-kilometre sprint.

"All in all it was an awesome race," said the soaking-wet LeGuellec, whose performance was a huge jump from his 61st-place showing at the 2006 Olympics in Turin. The result was the best ever for a Canadian competitor in men's biathlon.

FREESTYLE SKIING GOLD

Alexandre Bilodeau wraps himself in the Canadian flag after winning the gold medal in the men's moguls. Bilodeau edged out Dale Begg-Smith of Australia by 0.17 of a point.
(Sean Kilpatrick/The Canadian Press)

FREESTYLE SKIING GOLD

Alexandre Bilodeau performs a jump during his gold medal-winning moguls run. (Darryl Dyck/The Canadian Press)

SPEEDSKATING BRONZE

Kristina Groves displays the bronze medal she won in the women's 3,000-metre final. Daniela Anschutz Thoms of Germany, skating in the final pairing, seemed poised to nudge Groves from the podium, but fell short by three one-hundredths of a second.

(Ryan Remiorz/The Canadian Press)

SPEEDSKATING

Cindy Klassen, 30, competes in the women's 3,000-metre long-track race. The Winnipeg-born skater, winner of five medals at Turin in 2006, placed 14th in the final, but was cheered on by an enthusiastic crowd at the Richmond Olympic Oval.

(Nathan Denette/The Canadian Press)

BIATHLON

Jean-Philippe LeGuellec races through a snow squall en route to a sixth-place finish — the best ever by a Canadian male biathlete — in the men's 10-kilometre sprint.

(Andrew Vaughan/The Canadian Press)

LUGE

Ian Cockerline of Calgary puts on the brakes after his final run of the men's singles competition. Cockerline placed 20th, while teammates Sam Edney and Jeff Christie finished 7th and 14th respectively. (Frank Gunn/The Canadian Press)

DAY 4

MEMORIAL FOR NODAR

A memorial service was held for Nodar Kumaritashvili, the Georgian luger who died on the track in Whistler during a training run. Members of the Georgian Olympic delegation, the International Olympic Committee and the Vancouver organizing committee gathered at a funeral home to bid farewell to the 21-year-old slider.

ONE LAST SKATE

With family and friends looking on, and with streaks of grey hair setting him apart from younger competitors, Mike Ireland of Winnipeg closed the book on his lengthy Olympic speedskating career. At 36, Ireland was the oldest athlete in the speedskating competition. He finished 16th in the men's 500-metre long-track race. Ireland competed in four Olympics, but never won a medal. His best result in the 500 metres was seventh, in both 2002 and 2006.

BLAZING A TRAIL

Vanessa James had two reasons to feel proud on the ice: she was part of the first black figure skating pair in Olympic history, and it happened in the country of her birth. Skating for France, Toronto-born James and partner Yannick Bonheur were the first black skaters to reach these heights as part of a pair. They placed 14th.

Glory and disappointment

BY JAMES MCCARTEN

ONCE ALEXANDRE Bilodeau had set the gold standard, silver was never going to shine as brightly.

But that didn't seem to bother Mike Robertson.

The 24-year-old from Canmore, Alta., had first place in the snowboard cross in his sights, but ended up with silver after U.S. rival Seth Wescott — who also won gold in 2006 — sailed past him off a ramp near the bottom, eking out the win at the finish.

"It was kind of bittersweet," Robertson admitted after the race. "Obviously I wanted to win, for sure, but I'm so happy to be second. It's amazing."

Earlier in the day, Bilodeau beamed from atop the podium before thousands of screaming fans as he was presented with the first gold medal ever awarded to a Canadian athlete on home soil.

"I'm probably going to be in Trivial Pursuit," the 22-year-old moguls master from Rosemère, Que., said before the ceremony. "I can't believe it yet."

Hélène Daneault, mayor of Bilodeau's hometown northwest of Montreal, was among hundreds wearing red scarves emblazoned with "Good luck, Alexandre." She promised a massive party when the newly minted national hero comes home next month.

Disappointments in both the men's downhill and at the speedskating oval countered the thrill of Bilodeau's medal.

At the Richmond Olympic Oval, veteran speedskater Jeremy Wotherspoon of Red Deer, Alta., skated to an unsatisfying ninth-place finish in the 500 metres, well back of gold medallist Mo Tae-Bum of South Korea.

"I'd say the most disappointing thing is wondering if I have it in me anymore," Wotherspoon said. "That was the first thing that popped into my mind after that race."

Jamie Gregg of Edmonton was the top Canadian, in eighth. At one point, it was questionable whether the two-race event would be completed after an electric-powered ice-resurfacing machine littered the ice with snow and water for a second straight day.

In Whistler, Canada's showing in the long-delayed men's downhill was less than stellar. Erik Guay of Mont-Tremblant, Que., was the top Canadian, in fifth place, the country's best Olympic downhill result since 1998. But Manuel Osborne-Paradis of Invermere, B.C., who had been seen as Canada's top medal threat in the marquee event on

SKELETON

Amy Gough of Calgary speeds over the Olympic rings during women's skeleton training at the Whistler Sliding Centre.

(Jeff McIntosh/The Canadian Press)

the alpine skiing schedule, placed 17th, well back of gold medallist Didier Defago of Switzerland.

"It felt like I let the country down," said a dismayed Robbie Dixon, a Whistler native who crashed during his run.

At the Pacific Coliseum, spills seemed to be the order of the day for the Olympic pairs figure skating long program.

The first hint of trouble for Canada's favourites, Jessica Dubé and Bryce Davison, came in the warmup. Dubé shook her hands vigorously as if trying to snap herself into focus. A performance that started out shaky unravelled further for the Canadians, who finished sixth after Dubé fell while attempting her triple Salchow.

Even four-time Olympians Shen Xue and Zhao Hongbo, who finally captured gold after coming out of retirement for one last shot at Olympic glory, weren't perfect. Shen lost her balance on an overhead lift and slipped down Zhao's back.

SNOWBOARD SILVER

Seth Wescott of the U.S. passes Canada's Mike Robertson near the end of the course to claim the gold medal during the men's snowboard cross final at Cypress Mountain.

(Darryl Dyck/The Canadian Press)

HOCKEY

Goalie Martin Brodeur of the New Jersey
Devils rests on the bench during a men's
hockey practice on the eve of Team Canada's
opening game against Norway.

(Nathan Denette/The Canadian Press)

CROSS-COUNTRY SKIING

Alex Harvey of St-Ferréol-les-Neiges, Que., competes in men's 15-kilometre free cross-country skiing at Whistler Olympic Park. The 21-year-old placed 11th, while teammate Ivan Babikov of Canmore, Alta., finished eighth.

(Andrew Vaughan/The Canadian Press)

FIGURE SKATING

Jessica Dubé and Bryce Davison perform their free program in the pairs competition at the Pacific Coliseum. The pair hoped to reach the podium, but their combined score after the short program and free skate ranked them sixth overall. (Paul Chiasson/The Canadian Press)

FREESTYLE SKIING GOLD

The flags of the United States, Canada and Australia are raised during the playing of "O Canada" at the medal ceremony at B.C. Place on Feb. 15. Men's moguls gold medallist Alexandre Bilodeau is joined on the podium by silver medallist Dale Begg-Smith of Australia and bronze medallist Bryon Wilson of the U.S.

(Jonathan Hayward/The Canadian Press)

FIGURE SKATING

Cody Hay throws his partner, Anabelle Langlois, in the air during the pairs free skate. Participating in their first Olympics, the duo finished ninth.

(Paul Chiasson/The Canadian Press)

DAY 5

STYLE POINTS

What crowd-pleasing figure skater Johnny Weir lacked in points in the men's short program, he made up for in style. Wearing a flamboyant, translucent black suit adorned with pink trim and tassles, Weir skated a confident routine that engaged the crowd, then blew them a kiss and picked up a black, heart-shaped pillow with his name embroidered in pink.

MORE MISFORTUNE FOR JACOBELLIS

Lindsey Jacobellis of the U.S., who missed out on snowboard-cross gold in 2006 when a showboating stunt on the last jump caused her to crash, went home empty-handed again after a slip-up in the semifinals that caused her to veer off course. She placed fifth in the final rankings.

A FAST FAREWELL

On her last run in her last race in her last Olympics, Regan Lauscher whipped down the Whistler luge track like a laser beam at a dizzying 134 km/h, but still managed to stop and smell the roses. "As much as I could, I didn't look at the ice," said the 29-year-old slider from Red Deer, Alta. "I just felt it."

Hat tricks and setbacks

BY JAMES MCCARTEN

A GOLD medal in snowboard cross, a Jarome Iginla hat trick and an effortless shutout by hometown goaltender Roberto Luongo helped soothe jangled nerves on Day 5, amid some allegations that Canada's Olympics had gone glitchy.

Maëlle Ricker, 31, soared into the hearts of her hometown fans in West Vancouver as she survived a slippery, foggy afternoon on Cypress Mountain to give Canada another trip to the top of the podium.

Ricker, looking for redemption after a concussive fall in the final four years ago in Turin, Italy, led virtually wire to wire, leaving behind silver medallist Deborah Anthonioz of France and third-place finisher Olivia Nobs of Switzerland.

"It was such a motivator for me," a beaming Ricker said of her disappointment in 2006. "It made me work that much harder."

For Canadian hockey fans, however, there was only one event that really mattered.

Despite a scoreless first period, the men's hockey squad handed Norway an 8-0 loss, much to the delight of a rabid sellout crowd, clad head to toe in red and white, that showered the ice with hats when Iginla notched his third goal of the night.

The hockey win and Ricker's gold were the bright spots in a day that was otherwise dominated by talk of Vancouver's "Glitch Games" and the efforts of organizers to make sure the sobriquet didn't stick.

From weather aggravations to cancelled tickets to a controversy over the Olympic torch cauldron, organizers had been plagued by setbacks. At the Richmond Olympic Oval, officials gave up on the fleet of Olympia ice-resurfacing machines that had damaged the ice and delayed speedskating events and arranged for a Zamboni brand machine to be shipped from Calgary.

"It's a little like losing your luggage," spokeswoman Renée Smith-Valade said of the setbacks. "It's not whether the luggage gets lost — it's how you deal with it."

At the Pacific Coliseum, Russian figure skater Evgeni Plushenko came back from retirement in stunning fashion, finishing first in the men's short program with a routine that included one of his trademark quad jumps. Patrick Chan of Toronto struggled, ending the night in seventh.

There was also drama in curling when Kevin Martin's Canadian rink jumped out to a 5-1 lead over Norway,

SNOWBOARD GOLD

Maëlle Ricker holds up a Canadian flag after winning the gold medal in women's snowboard cross. Teammate Dominique Maltais of Petite-Rivière-St-François, Que., a bronze medallist at Turin in 2006, didn't qualify for the quarter-finals. (Sean Kilpatrick/The Canadian Press)

skipped by Thomas Ulsrud, only to be forced to eke out a 7-6 win in extra ends.

On the women's side, Cheryl Bernard claimed her first victory of the Games by drawing to the house with her final stone as thousands of raucous fans showered her with deafening applause. Bernard knocked off the team led by two-time Games silver medallist Mirjam Ott of Switzerland, 5-4, in the 10th end, closing out the match to a boisterous ovation.

SNOWBOARD GOLD

Maëlle Ricker makes a turn during a qualifying run in the women's snowboard cross. Ricker won her quarter-final and semifinal heats by comfortable margins before winning the gold medal.

(Sean Kilpatrick/The Canadian Press)

LUGE

Regan Lauscher lowers her visor before her third run of the women's singles luge competition at Whistler. Lauscher was the top Canadian in the event, finishing 15th. Alex Gough of Calgary was 18th, while fellow Calgarian Meaghan Simister was 25th.

(Jacques Boissinot/The Canadian Press)

HOCKEY

Canadian fans celebrate their men's hockey team's 8-0
victory over Norway. Jarome Iginla of the Calgary Flames
had a hat trick, while Sidney Crosby of the Pittsburgh
Penguins contributed three assists. Roberto Luongo of
the Vancouver Canucks recorded the shutout, stopping
15 shots. ((Ryan Remiorz/The Canadian Press))

FIGURE SKATING

Patrick Chan performs his short program in the men's competition at the Pacific Coliseum in Vancouver. Ranked ninth in the world entering the Olympics, the 19-year-old Toronto resident stood seventh after the short program.

(Robert Skinner/The Canadian Press)

THE WEATHER

Volunteers walk over a surface of snow packed atop hay bales at the bottom of the snowboarding course at Cypress Mountain in West Vancouver. On Feb. 16, organizers cancelled an additional 20,000 standing-room tickets for events at the troubled venue after rain and warm weather rendered those areas potentially unsafe.

(Darryl Dyck/The Canadian Press)

CURLING

Clad in their trademark multicoloured trousers, Norwegian skip Thomas Ulsrud (centre) and second Christoffer Svae (right) confer with coach Ole Ingvaldsen during a time out in men's curling action at the Vancouver Olympic Centre. Canadian skip Kevin Martin looks pensively down the ice.

(Nathan Denette/The Canadian Press)

DAY 6

SUCKING UP TO "SYRUP SUCKERS"

Stephen Colbert, who spent months poking fun at Canadians on his TV show *The Colbert Report* — calling them "syrup suckers" and "Saskatche-whiners" — arrived in Vancouver to extend an olive branch to his hosts, whom he described as "friendly and very easy to pander to."

CROSS-COUNTRY COURAGE

Petra Majdic of Slovenia was doubled over in pain and gasping for air after a spectacular crash during a training run for the women's individual sprint classic. She slid out of a slippery 180-degree corner, fell three metres off an embankment and landed in a gully. Majdic went on to battle her way to a bronze medal.

THEY CAN SEE CLEARLY NOW

Workers in Vancouver spent the night building a rooftop viewing platform and modifying the controversial chain-link fence that protected the outdoor Olympic cauldron in order to afford disgruntled spectators a better view — and the chance to take unobstructed photographs — of the flame.

The Americans invade

BY JAMES MCCARTEN

IT WAS a day of death-defying American determination, from the gold-medal grit of skier Lindsey Vonn to the gravity-cheating flight of snowboarder Shaun White.

Vonn, gnashing her teeth through a painful deep-tissue bruise on her shin, got things going early on an angry Whistler course that chewed up and spat out nearly a fifth of the field, but couldn't keep the gifted and telegenic downhill star from her date with destiny — and Olympic gold.

By nightfall came White, the only boarder in the Olympics with his very own video game, who put on a flame-haired display of halfpipe abandon, McTwisting his way to the top of the podium, his face obscured by goggles and a Stars-and-Stripes bandana like that of a radical bandit.

And in between, U.S. long-track speedskating star Shani Davis, 27, also demanded his share of the attention, lunging across the finish line in the men's 1,000 metres to the delight of comedian-cum-pseudo-psychologist Stephen Colbert.

It wasn't an entirely American party, however: Marianne St-Gelais of St-Félicien, Que., celebrated her 20th birthday by giving Canada the unexpected gift of silver in the women's 500 metres.

"I'm still the rookie, but I've made a name for myself," said the bubbly St-Gelais, who alternated between tears and giggles.

"I pushed myself to the limit and I went as far as possible."

For most of the day — brightened, at last, by a perfect blue sky in Whistler — the dominant story involved Vonn and her badly bruised leg, a training injury that at the start of the Games was billed as a potential race-killer but seemed almost an afterthought by the end of a bruising, crash-filled women's downhill.

"I got the gold medal that I came here to get," said Vonn, who conceded she was the beneficiary of weather delays that dogged the alpine events.

"That gave me a lot of extra time to heal my shin, and that's exactly what I needed. Someone was definitely looking out for me upstairs."

The perilous Whistler course sent more than a few racers careening and cartwheeling, skis akimbo, into the netting. Many crashes came after a massive jump near the bottom, nicknamed "Hot Air," which catapulted several competitors out of contention.

None of the six racers who crashed out were Canadian. Britt Janyk of Whistler was the top Canadian, in sixth.

In speedskating, Canada's potential medal haul shrank when Denny Morrison, 24, of Fort St. John, B.C., finished 13th behind Davis in the men's 1,000. Red Deer's Jeremy Wotherspoon, skating in his last Olympic event, was next, in 14th.

At Cypress Mountain, where White was shredding the halfpipe with his Double McTwist 1260 (two flips while doing three-and-a-half rotations), his Canadian counterparts were among the ranks of the shreddees. Justin Lamoureux of Ottawa, 33, the only one to make it to the final, finished well back of the leaders.

SHORT-TRACK SPEEDSKATING SILVER

Marianne St-Gelais celebrates after winning the silver medal in the women's 500 metres. She edged out bronze medallist Arianna Fontana of Italy by less than a tenth of a second.

(Paul Chiasson/The Canadian Press)

ALPINE SKIING

Anja Paerson of Sweden falls near the finish line during the women's downhill. She was one of six skiers who crashed on the course at Whistler and failed to complete their runs.

(Gero Breloer/The Associated Press)

SHORT-TRACK SPEEDSKATING SILVER

Lowering her left hand to keep her balance, Marianne St-Gelais leans into a turn during a women's 500-metre quarter-final heat at the Pacific Coliseum. British skater Elise Christie is close behind. (Paul Chiasson/The Canadian Press)

HOLD IT... GOT IT!

From a rooftop observation deck overlooking the Olympic cauldron in Jack Poole Square, visitors take photographs and pose for pictures.
(Graeme Roy/The Canadian Press)

HOCKEY

Sarah Vaillancourt (26) is congratulated by teammates after scoring a goal in the first period of Team Canada's preliminary-round game against Sweden at UBC Thunderbird Arena. Canada went on to win 13-1 as it sailed into the quarter-finals. Meghan Agosta led the team with three goals and two assists, while team captain Hayley Wickenheiser chipped in a goal and four assists. (Scott Gardner/The Canadian Press)

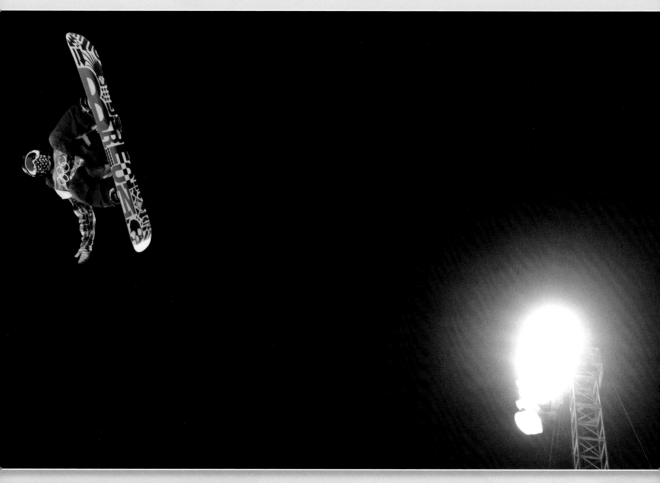

SNOWBOARD

Shaun White of the U.S. twists and flips his way through the night air during his gold medal-winning run in the men's halfpipe at Cypress Mountain. (Darryl Dyck/The Canadian Press)

ALPINE SKIING

Lindsey Vonn of the U.S. races down the slope at Whistler, en route to a gold medal in the women's downhill. She became the first American woman ever to win Olympic gold in downhill skiing. Teammate Julia Mancuso won silver. (Frank Gunn/The Canadian Press)

ALPINE SKIING

Britt Janyk of Whistler posted the fastest time by a Canadian in the women's downhill final, finishing sixth. Emily Brydon of Fernie, B.C., placed 16th, while Shona Rubens of Canmore, Alta., was 21st.

(Alessandro Trovati/The Associated Press)

LUGE

As Chris Moffat (front) puts on the brakes, his brother Mike stands and raises his arms in celebration at the end of their run in the men's doubles. The pair finished seventh, an improvement of two slots over their result in Turin in 2006. Canada's second team — Justin Snith and Tristan Walker, both 18 — placed 15th in their first Olympic final. (Jacques Boissinot/The Canadian Press)

DAY 7

LEASING THE LAURELS?

American snowboarder Nate Holland apparently wasn't kidding when he said the U.S. would "rent" the medals podium out from under the Canadian bid to own it. A week into the games, the U.S. was leading in medals and in contention to win both the total and gold-medal counts.

A COSTLY POINT

Canada's 3-2 victory over the Swiss men's hockey team came at a price. Points earned in the preliminary round affected teams' seedings in later rounds. By winning in a shootout rather than in regulation time, Team Canada received just two points instead of three.

TUNEFUL TRIBUTE

Some of rock music's most esteemed names gathered on the stage at the Queen Elizabeth Theatre for a tribute to Canadian music legend Neil Young. Among the luminaries on the bill were former Velvet Underground frontman Lou Reed, new-wave pioneer Elvis Costello and Canadian singer-songwriter Ron Sexsmith.

Winning — by a whisker

BY JAMES MCCARTEN

CHRISTINE NESBITT couldn't believe she had won. And Canadians couldn't believe their hockey team nearly didn't.

Gold-medal glory almost turned to grief as Nesbitt's long-track speedskating medal in the women's 1,000 metres was upstaged by a nerve-racking men's hockey game that was far closer than it should have been.

Sidney Crosby scored in a shootout to finally dispatch stubborn Switzerland, the same country that, four years ago to the day, upset Team Canada 2-0 in Turin — a forgettable Olympics for Canadian hockey fans, who watched their heroes finish a dismal seventh.

"I looked forward to that chance and am glad I made the most of it," Crosby said of the goal.

The pride of Cole Harbour, N.S., beat Swiss goaltender Jonas Hiller of the Anaheim Ducks on his second shootout attempt, giving Canada a 3-2 victory.

The game very nearly tarnished the gleam of Nesbitt's gold, which she claimed by not quite the narrowest of margins — two one-hundredths of a second — in what she later described as a less-than-illustrious performance.

"I couldn't believe it," said the 24-year-old from London, Ont., who looked stunned as she accepted hugs and accolades after the race and sheepish as she ascended the podium during the flower ceremony. "I did not think it was good enough."

Dutch skaters Annette Gerritsen and Laurine van Riessen claimed silver and bronze. Kristina Groves, who won bronze in the 3,000 metres, finished fourth — missing out on another medal by six one-hundredths of a second.

By nightfall, the focus was on the thrills, spills and frills of the men's free skate, where 25-year-old Evan Lysacek of Chicago delivered a brilliant long program to thwart Russian skating czar Evgeni Plushenko's bid for the first back-to-back golds in 58 years. Clad in a black Vera Wang suit that featured a pair of jewel-encrusted snakes, Lysacek, the reigning world champion, skated a rousing routine set to *Scheherazade* that brought the crowd to its feet.

Plushenko claimed the silver, although after congratulating bronze medallist Daisuke Takahashi of Japan, he briefly hopped up to the top of the podium, a mischievous glint in his eye, before stepping down to the second-place position.

Patrick Chan of Toronto started strong, but stepped out of the landing on his triple Lutz and fell on his second triple Axel, finishing in fifth. "The best part was not the marks, it was just the crowd — the Canadian crowd and the passion that they show for their athletes," the 19-year-old said afterward.

Lysacek's win gave U.S. figure-skating fans further reason to embrace Canada: it was the first gold-medal win for an American skater since Brian Boitano edged out Brian Orser at the 1988 Games in Calgary.

Gold medallist Christine Nesbitt is flanked by Dutch speedskaters Annette Gerritsen (left) and Laurine van Riessen (right) during the medal ceremony for the women's long-track 1,000 metres.

(Adrian Wyld/The Canadian Press)

SPEEDSKATING GOLD

Christine Nesbitt skates with
the Canadian flag after winning
the gold medal in the women's
1,000-metre long-track competition
at the Richmond Olympic Oval.

(Adrian Wyld/The Canadian Press)

SNOWBOARD

Mercedes Nicoll of Whistler, B.C., rides up the wall of the pipe during the women's halfpipe semifinals. Nicoll earned a spot in the finals, where she placed sixth. (Sean Kilpatrick/The Canadian Press)

CURLING

Team Canada skip Cheryl Bernard throws her rock as lead Cori Bartel (centre) and second Carolyn Darbyshire prepare to sweep in a round-robin match against Germany. The Canadians required extra ends to win 6-5.

(Nathan Denette/The Canadian Press)

BIATHLON

Jean-Philippe LeGuellec nears the finish line in the men's 20-kilometre individual race. LeGuellec, the sole Canadian in the event, placed 13th.

(Andrew Vaughan/The Canadian Press)

HOCKEY

Goaltender Martin Brodeur (left) and Sidney Crosby celebrate Team Canada's 3-2 shootout win over Switzerland in the preliminary round of men's hockey at Canada Hockey Place. Crosby scored the winning goal, while Brodeur saved all four Swiss shootout attempts.
(Jonathan Hayward/The Canadian Press)

SKELETON

Jeff Pain of Calgary leaps onto his sled to start a run during the men's skeleton heats at Whistler Sliding Centre. His helmet bears the image of a "raging beaver." (Jeff McIntosh/The Canadian Press)

1   2   3   4   5   6   8

SNOWBOARD

Sarah Conrad of Dartmouth, N.S., airs out of the pipe during the women's halfpipe qualifying runs at Cypress Mountain. Conrad was 18th in the final rankings, while teammate Mercedes Nicoll of Whistler, B.C., was sixth and Palmer Taylor of Collingwood, Ont., was 26th in her Olympic debut.

(Sean Kilpatrick/The Canadian Press)

FIGURE SKATING

Evan Lysacek of the U.S. raises his arms in triumph after completing his free skate at the Pacific Coliseum. Lysacek edged out the defending Olympic and European champion, Evgeni Plushenko of Russia, to capture the gold medal. (Mark Baker/The Associated Press)

DAY 8

PAINFUL TRIP TO THE PODIUM

Cross-country skier Petra Majdic of Slovenia had to be helped to the podium to receive her bronze medal in the women's individual sprint classic. She didn't learn the extent of the injuries she suffered during a training run — four fractured ribs and a collapsed lung — until after the finals.

ELVIS IS IN THE BUILDING ...

Figure skating fans were still buzzing about American Evan Lysacek — did he deserve the gold medal, even though he didn't attempt a quadruple jump? Or was the Quad King, silver medallist Evgeni Plushenko of Russia, robbed? Three-time world champion Elvis Stojko weighed in: "Sorry, Evan Lysacek. You're a great skater and all. But that wasn't Olympic champion material." But Jeffrey Buttle, the 2008 world champion, disagreed. "There's just not a lot of substance to (Plushenko's) program," he said.

... BUT IS STEPHEN?

It looked as though Stephen Colbert had left Vancouver. Or had he? "Vancouverage" of the Olympics for his TV show *The Colbert Report* was to be filmed in a "coverage chamber" complete with stone fireplace and a view of the mountains. In New York, right? Said Colbert: "I can neither confirm nor deny that reality."

Underdog becomes top dog

BY JAMES MCCARTEN

CANADIANS LOVE an underdog. Now, they love Jon Montgomery even more.

The ebullient, fast-talking auctioneer and car salesman from Russell, Man., wasn't predicted to reach the heights that he did in men's skeleton as he pounced atop the podium as a gold medallist and yelled, "We're No. 1, baby!"

That spot had been reserved for Mellisa Hollingsworth, the 29-year-old from Eckville, Alta., who could only hang her head in dismay after her dreams of Olympic glory were decimated by a bumpy final run that dropped her from second place to fifth.

"It is just really hard," Hollingsworth said, her cheeks stained with tears. "I feel like I have let my entire country down."

In a bizarre twist that added insult to injury, Michael Douglas, 38, of Toronto was disqualified from the men's finals when he failed to deliver his sled for an official post-race inspection before the prescribed deadline.

The men's downhillers were shut out of the super giant slalom, won by Aksel Lund Svindal of Norway. American rivals Bode Miller and Andrew Weibrecht took silver and bronze, raising the U.S. medal count to 20.

Erik Guay of Mont-Tremblant, Que., was top Canadian in fifth, missing a podium finish by just three one-hundredths of a second. "It's tough to swallow," Guay admitted. "I could have easily been there."

Teammate Manuel Osborne-Paradis, 26, of Invermere, B.C., crashed out of what became another spill-filled race, as did 25-year-old Whistler native Robbie Dixon.

Aside from Montgomery's medal, another highlight on the day for Canada came from curler Cheryl Bernard, who endured against Denmark to prevail 5-4 in an extra end and preserve her perfect record at the Vancouver Games. "The games are a little bit tight, probably too tight for everyone in our family," Bernard said later.

And a third bright spot came in the compulsory dance portion of the ice dancing competition.

Medal hopefuls Tessa Virtue of London, Ont., and Scott Moir of Ilderton, Ont., found themselves in second place after their Tango Romantica.

SKELETON GOLD

Jon Montgomery celebrates his gold medal in men's skeleton. Montgomery edged out Martins Dukurs, who led the World Cup standings entering the Olympics, by seven one-hundredths of a second. (Jeff McIntosh/The Canadian Press)

The Canadians left nothing to chance in their preparation for the compulsory dance, flying in Elena Tchaikovskaya, the legendary coach who conceived the dance in 1974, to their training base in the week before arriving in Vancouver.

"The passion and energy she brought was just incredible," Virtue said.

FIGURE SKATING

Tessa Virtue and Scott Moir skate their way to a second-place finish in the compulsory portion of the ice dance.

(Paul Chiasson/The Canadian Press)

SKELETON GOLD

Jon Montgomery slides into the finish area after his gold medal-winning run. (Frank Gunn/The Canadian Press)

ALPINE SKIING

Peter Fill of Italy crashes near the end of his
run in the men's super giant slalom. Although
he crossed the finish line, he and two other
skiers were disqualified for missing gates.
Another 15 competitors, including Manuel
Osborne-Paradis and Robbie Dixon of
Canada, failed to complete their runs.

(Jacques Boissinot/The Canadian Press)

SKELETON

Mellisa Hollingsworth crosses the finish line after her disappointing final run in the women's skeleton. Hollingsworth hit a wall in one of the early turns, slowing her down and eliminating her from medal contention.

(Frank Gunn/The Canadian Press)

FREESTYLE SKIING

Sarah Ainsworth of Britain soars through
the air during women's aerials training.

(Darryl Dyck/The Canadian Press)

READY FOR A CLOSE-UP

Sporting some snakelike headgear, a spectator photographs the action during the men's super giant slalom.

(Matthew McCarthy/The Canadian Press)

FREESTYLE SKIING

Michael Schmid (left) of Switzerland and Errol Kerr of Jamaica soar through the air off a jump during a ski-cross training run at Cypress Mountain. (Darryl Dyck/The Canadian Press)

ALPINE SKIING

Aksel Lund Svindal of Norway reacts — apparently with delight — after his gold medal-winning run in the men's super giant slalom.

(Jacques Boissinot/The Canadian Press)

DAY 9

NICE SONG, BUT THE PHOTO?

The word "bashful" was just not in the vocabulary of gold medallist Jon Montgomery. At the medals ceremony, he did his trademark standing leap onto the podium, then belted out "O Canada," which he described as "a song you can sing all day." He admitted, however, that he was embarrassed by a TV network's shirtless promotional picture of him, taken during training. "I sure hope that they pull that one," he said. "I wasn't in the best shape We'd spent a bit of time at the end of last season enjoying our downtime, shall I say."

MEDAL HOPES DASHED

Lyndon Rush crashed in his second run, effectively erasing any Canadian medal hopes in the two-man bobsled. "Awwwww, geeeez!" shouted fellow Canadian pilot Pierre Lueders, who rushed over to see Rush and brakeman Lascelles Brown skidding up the outrun, their overturned sled scraping the track and sending up a spray of snow. "Man, oh, man, you don't want to see this at all," Lueders said later. "Especially teammates. It's horrible." Rush and Brown, who were in medal contention before the crash, marched forlornly up the hill to be examined by doctors.

Bleak Saturday

BY DONALD MCKENZIE

THE MOMENTUM just never materialized.

A day after a brash Jon Montgomery lifted Canadians out of their seats with an electrifying gold-medal performance in men's skeleton, none of the country's Olympic athletes was able to emulate the native of Russell, Man. — or even reach the podium.

The shutout broke a seven-day streak of medals for Canada and pushed the host team down a rung in the medal standings.

Perhaps the biggest disappointment was the failure of both Charles Hamelin and his brother François to come through in the men's 1,000-metre short-track speedskating final. Charles' fourth-place finish earned him nothing more than bragging rights over his brother in the five-man final.

Charles said the loud Pacific Coliseum crowd threw him off initially. "It meant that at the beginning of the race I had trouble pacing my speed," he said. "I was going too fast in the beginning and it meant that at the end I didn't have the legs to place on the podium."

At the Richmond Olympic Oval, long-track speedskater Denny Morrison tired badly at the end of the 1,500-metre final and finished a distant ninth — the second straight frustrating performance for the native of Fort St. John, B.C., after his 13th-place finish in Wednesday's 1,000.

"That's kind of what's been happening to me all season long," said Morrison. "I don't know if it's something with the program or what, because I know as far as lactic capacity or total lactic power is concerned, if we were to do hill sprints I could crush all these guys."

Dutchman Mark Tuitert won the gold, Shani Davis of the United States took silver and Havard Bokko of Norway finished third.

The weak result for the speedskaters followed a poor day for Canadians in skiing events at Whistler, where competitors failed to qualify in the women's aerials final and also lagged badly in the super-G as Andrea Fischbacher of Austria denied American Lindsey Vonn a sweep of the speed events.

The lone morsel of good news for Canada on the otherwise dreary day was Kevin Martin finally getting the better of Britain's David Murdoch in men's curling after losing four consecutive times to the current world champion. But breaking the streak wasn't easy; Martin required two points in the 10th to eke out a 7-6 victory that ran his record to 6-0.

BOBSLED

Lyndon Rush and Lascelles Brown slide upside down after crashing during their second run at Whistler. The crash dropped the pair from third to 21st in the standings. Aside from a few cuts on Rush's left hand, both men were unharmed. (Jeff McIntosh/The Canadian Press)

Martin and his rink may have received a boost from a patriotic crowd that burst into an impromptu rendition of "O Canada" shortly after the 10th end had begun.

"The national anthem," said Martin. "Wasn't that something? They were even in tune and probably 5,000 strong singing it. Something you'll remember for the rest of your life."

Outside the Olympic venues, Games officials struggled to cope with the biggest crowds so far in Vancouver, flooding the city's downtown and raising security concerns. Police closed liquor stores in a bid to curb over-enthusiastic celebrations.

ALPINE SKIING

Georgia Simmerling of West Vancouver, B.C., sails past a gate during her run in the women's super giant slalom final. Simmerling finished 27th, while teammate Britt Janyk was 17th. Emily Brydon crashed and did not finish.

(Frank Gunn/The Canadian Press)

FREESTYLE SKIING

Veronika Bauer of Toronto tries to correct her landing during a qualifying jump in the women's aerials. She placed 15th, failing to advance to the finals.

(Tara Walton/The Canadian Press)

SKELETON

Jon Montgomery (centre) appears atop the podium — and on big-screen displays — during the awards ceremony in Whistler. He is flanked by Alexander Tretyakov of Russia (left) and silver medallist Martin Dukurs of Latvia.

(Boris Minkevich/The Canadian Press)

HOCKEY

Hayley Wickenheiser, captain of the women's team, watches from the bench during a Team Canada practice.

(Rick Eglinton/The Canadian Press)

CROSS-COUNTRY SKIING

Ivan Babikov of Canmore, Alta., skis to a
fifth-place finish in the men's 30-kilometre
pursuit, the best result by a Canadian. George
Grey was eighth, Alex Harvey placed ninth
and Devon Kershaw was 16th.

(Andrew Vaughan/The Canadian Press)

SPEEDSKATING

A dejected Denny Morrison sits on a bench after placing ninth in the men's long-track 1,500 metres. Mathieu Giroux of Pointe-aux-Trembles, Que., was 14th, Lucas Makowsky of Regina was 19th and Kyle Parrott of Richmond, B.C., finished 37th.

(Adrian Wyld/The Canadian Press)

SHORT-TRACK SPEEDSKATING

François Hamelin leads Lee Ho-Suk of Korea (left) and Latvia's Haralds Silovs during the quarter-finals of the men's short-track 1,000 metres. Hamelin came in fifth in the final. (Paul Chiasson/The Canadian Press)

SKI JUMPING

Simon Ammann of Switzerland takes off from the long-hill jump during men's individual competition.
(Jeff McIntosh/The Canadian Press)

PARTY CENTRAL (pages 106-107)

Thousands of revellers fill Robson Square in downtown Vancouver, which became a focal point for celebrations during the Games.
(Robert Skinner/The Canadian Press)

DAY 10

TRAGIC NEWS

Figure skater Joannie Rochette wiped away tears, took a deep breath and stepped onto the Pacific Coliseum ice to practise, seven hours after getting the news that her mother and No. 1 fan, Thérèse Rochette, had died of a heart attack in a Vancouver hospital. Rochette, 24, from Île-Dupas, Que., decided to compete as planned in the Olympics, seeking comfort in the place she knew best — the rink.

STICKS + SANDBAGS = SUCCESS

Ice dancers Moir, 22, and Virtue, 20, weren't ruffled by the nerves that caused other young Canadians, such as Patrick Chan, to falter at their first Olympics. Even more remarkable was that Virtue underwent surgery to relieve chronic pain in her shins and spent the fall before the Winter Games in rehab. Moir, in her absence, trained with hockey sticks and a sandbag.

HOMETOWN SUPPORT

Speedskater Cindy Klassen may have finished 21st in the 1,500 metres, but she was still golden in her hometown of Winnipeg, where family and fans gathered at an outdoor rink to watch TV screens as she competed. Klassen, a five-time medallist in 2006, missed the entire 2008-09 season to recover from surgery on both knees.

Not-so-super Sunday

BY JAMES MCCARTEN

IT WAS an upset, all right — and an upsetting one at that.

Spectacular goaltending from Ryan Miller, combined with a sluggish performance at the other end of the ice from rival netminder Martin Brodeur, conspired to break the hearts of Canadian hockey fans Sunday as Canada lost 5-3 to the U.S.

A roiling sea of spectators, decked out in jerseys, mittens, scarves and toques despite Vancouver's unseasonal warmth, gathered in bars, restaurants and city streets to watch the game.

But instead of the strong performance they hoped for, their heroes delivered a middling effort while Brian Rafalski scored two goals and Ryan Miller made 42 saves to help the Americans prevail in what was otherwise a wildly entertaining hockey game.

When Sidney Crosby scored to bring the Canadians within a goal in the dying minutes of the third period, the crowd watching the game outdoors on two massive big-screen displays hollered and squealed with renewed vigour.

Minutes later, however, an empty-net goal by the U.S. left them deflated. The roar was replaced by the sound of empty water bottles and crushed-up soda cans rattling on the pavement underfoot.

The joy was gone, but hope persisted.

"Canada played hard," said Brandon Hill of Ladysmith, B.C. "They just about had it, but all in all, the Americans, they were the better team. We can still win the gold medal."

Canadians had to look elsewhere for reasons to cheer, and found them in ice dancers Tessa Virtue and Scott Moir, who delivered an inspired Spanish flamenco in the original dance program Sunday to grab hold of first place going into the final segment, the free dance.

"That moment we'll never forget for the rest of our life," Moir said afterward. "I don't think a piece of metal around my neck is going to make it any better."

Long-track speedskater Kristina Groves helped boost Canada's medal count with a second-place showing in the women's 1,500 metres. Groves won bronze in the 3,000 metres last week, making her the first Canadian athlete to win multiple medals in Vancouver.

In curling, undefeated Canadian skip Kevin Martin claimed his seventh straight match, this time against

Markus Eggler of Switzerland, clinching the top seed in the semifinals.

Women's skip Cheryl Bernard, scheduled to play two games, wasn't so lucky. Her rink dropped a 6-5 extra-end decision to Wang Bingyu of China after thrashing the Americans 9-2 earlier in the day. Bernard stressed that her rink could take some positives from the defeat.

"Sometimes it's a good kick in the you-know to get you moving and not get complacent," she said.

Kristina Groves (left), the silver medallist in the women's long-track 1,500 metres, celebrates her second trip to the podium. Ireen Wust of the Netherlands (centre) won gold, while Martina Sablikova of the Czech Republic took the bronze.

(Robert Skinner/The Canadian Press)

BIATHLON

In a chaotic mass of skis and poles, athletes in the men's 15-kilometre mass start cast lengthy shadows over the snow at Whistler. Jean-Philippe LeGuellec, the first Canadian ever to compete in the Olympics at this distance, placed 30th.

(Andrew Vaughan/The Canadian Press)

FIGURE SKATING

Russian ice dancers Oksana Domnina and Maxim Shabalin perform their original dance, dressed in costumes similar to those that drew criticism from Aboriginal people in Australia. (Paul Chiasson/The Canadian Press)

FIGURE SKATING

Joannie Rochette (right), still shaken by the news of her mother's death, speaks with her coach, Manon Perron, during a practice session.

(Paul Chiasson/The Canadian Press)

FREESTYLE SKIING

Christopher Del Bosco of Sudbury, Ont., loses control and crashes during men's ski cross. In third place at the time, Del Bosco was making an unsuccessful bid to capture the lead. He finished fourth.

(Darryl Dyck/The Canadian Press)

ALPINE SKIING

Ryan Semple of Montreal races in the downhill portion of the men's super combined. He was the top Canadian, finishing 15th. Michael Janyk of Whistler, B.C., was 26th, Louis-Pierre Hélie of Berthierville, Que., was 30th and Tyler Nella of Burlington, Ont., was 32nd. (Jacques Boissinot/The Canadian Press)

FIGURE SKATING

Ice dancer Tessa Virtue of London, Ont., hugs partner Scott Moir of nearby Ilderton, Ont., after their original dance. (Paul Chiasson/The Canadian Press)

HOCKEY

Canada's Sidney Crosby tumbles over American goaltender Ryan Miller and into the net during preliminary-round action at Canada Hockey Place. Bryan Rafalski of the Detroit Red Wings had two goals and an assist to pace Team USA to a 5-3 victory. (Jonathan Hayward/The Canadian Press)

HOCKEY

Canadian goaltender Martin Brodeur (left) congratulates his American counterpart, Ryan Miller, after their game. (Jonathan Hayward/The Canadian Press)

CYPRESS SUNRISE

The sun rises over the Fraser Valley as a ski-cross athlete rides the chair lift on his way to inspect the course at Cypress Mountain.

(Sean Kilpatrick/The Canadian Press)

CURLING

Canadian skip Cheryl Bernard considers her team's next move while Chinese skip Wang Bingyu looks on. Canada came back from an early 3-0 deficit, but lost the round-robin match 6-5 in an extra end. (Rick Eglinton/The Canadian Press)

DAY 11

MEDAL SHORTAGE

The ice-dancing gold was Canada's 10th medal — nowhere near enough for Canada to dominate the medals table, the stated objective of the five-year, $117-million Own the Podium program. "We are going to be short of our goal," Chris Rudge, chief executive of the Canadian Olympic Committee, conceded at a news conference.

CANADIAN WOMEN ADVANCE

At Canada Hockey Place, the Canadian women's hockey team extended their winning streak with a decisive 5-0 semifinal victory over Finland, securing a berth in the gold-medal game against the U.S. No one, however, was taking the American women for granted. "We're ready for anything that comes our way," said Canadian captain Hayley Wickenheiser.

CROSS-COUNTRY HIGHLIGHT

Alex Harvey of St-Ferréol-les-Neiges, Que., and Devon Kershaw of Sudbury, Ont., finished fourth in the men's team sprint, the best-ever result for Canadian men on an Olympic cross-country course. "Alex Harvey is the most talented skier I've ever, ever trained with, or raced with," Kershaw, 27, said of his 20-year-old teammate.

Golden dance, golden moment

BY JAMES MCCARTEN

FOR CANADIAN figure-skating fans, patience is a Virtue — and never Moir so than it was on Day 11 of the Games.

That was the day Canada discovered Olympic redemption in the gleaming smiles, sparkling sequins and smooth, effortless style of Tessa Virtue and Scott Moir as they delivered North America's first-ever gold medal in ice dancing.

After a fiery Spanish flamenco routine in the original dance segment — complete with handclaps, skate stomps and the swish of Virtue's red skirt — the southwestern Ontario pair closed the deal with a nearly flawless romantic program set to Gustav Mahler's *Symphony No. 5*.

Virtue wore a wispy white dress and a gleaming grin to match; Moir kept it classic with a billowy white shirt and black pants.

The highlight of the night was their breathtaking circus-performer lift known as the Goose. Virtue balanced on one knee on Moir's crouching back, her arms outstretched, before spilling into his arms.

Moir, ever the comedian, jokingly told Virtue they had won silver when the scores were first announced. She briefly believed him before realizing she'd been had and laughing it off.

Their training partners and close friends, Meryl Davis and Charlie White, came second. Oksana Domnina and Maxim Shabalin of Russia earned the bronze medal.

"Oh my God, it's the moment we've dreamed of," gushed Moir. "We couldn't be happier."

Virtue said the pair, partners for 13 years, knew they were ready. "We were confident in that. It was just about skating together and skating in our hearts and enjoying the moment for us and skating for the two of us. We're so proud to be Canadian and to do it for the nation."

The gold medal was the first in figure skating for Canada since Jamie Salé and David Pelletier shared the pairs title eight years ago in Salt Lake City.

In the original dance, Domnina and Shabalin went with the same oddly comical routine that raised eyebrows and prompted an outcry from Australian Aboriginal leaders when the pair skated it at the European championships in January.

FIGURE SKATING GOLD

Canadian ice dancers Tessa Virtue and Scott Moir display their gold medals after their free skate.

(Paul Chiasson/The Canadian Press)

The Russians wore dark nylon body suits with cartoonish loincloths, leaves and faux body paint. At points, a grinning Shabalin grabbed Domnina's ponytail as they clapped and bopped across the ice to music that included riffs from a didgeridoo.

Domnina and Shabalin were criticized for cultural theft not only by Aboriginal leaders in Australia but by First Nations leaders in B.C. They tried to make amends by consulting with both groups after the fact.

FREESTYLE SKIING

Julia Murray of Whistler, B.C., takes part in a women's ski cross training run at Cypress Mountain. In the background are two peaks known as The Lions. (Sean Kilpatrick/The Canadian Press)

FIGURE SKATING GOLD

Tessa Virtue and Scott Moir perform their gold medal-winning free dance in the ice-dance competition at the Pacific Coliseum. The pair began skating together in 1997, when Virtue was eight years old and Moir was 10. (Paul Chiasson/The Canadian Press)

BOBSLED

Helen Upperton, 30, of Calgary drives her bobsled down the track during a training run.

(Jeff McIntosh/The Canadian Press)

FREESTYLE SKIING

Steve Omischl, 31, of Kelowna, B.C., spins through the air in a qualifying run for the men's aerials.

(Sean Kilpatrick/The Canadian Press)

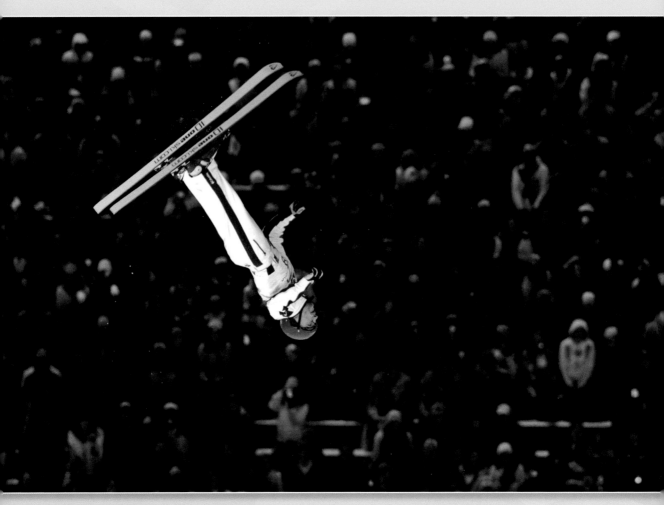

FREESTYLE SKIING

Canada's Warren Shouldice performs
a jump during men's aerials qualifying.
(Darryl Dyck/The Canadian Press)

HOCKEY

Marie-Philip Poulin (29) jumps into the arms of Caroline Ouellette after Ouellette's third-period goal against Finland. Team Canada won the semifinal game 5-0. (Jonathan Hayward/The Canadian Press)

FREESTYLE SKIING

Steve Omischl competes in men's aerials
qualifying. All three Canadians —
Omischl, Warren Shouldice and
Kyle Nissen — advanced to the finals.

(Darryl Dyck/The Canadian Press)

CURLING

Team Canada second Marc Kennedy (left) and lead Ben Hebert provide a study in concentration as they sweep during a match against the U.S. Canada won all eight of its round-robin matches to clinch the top seed in the semifinals. (Nathan Denette/The Canadian Press)

SKI JUMPING

Daiki Ito of Japan goes airborne during the team competition at Whistler Olympic Park. The Canadian team of Mackenzie Boyd-Clowes, Trevor Morrice, Eric Mitchell and Stefan Read did not qualify for the final.

(Jeff McIntosh/The Canadian Press)

CURLING

Canadian second Carolyn Darbyshire (left) and skip Cheryl Bernard acknowledge the cheers of the crowd after defeating Team Sweden, the reigning Olympic gold medallists, by a 6-2 score.

(Nathan Denette/The Canadian Press)

DAY 12

SWIFT SLEDDING

In the first women's bobsled heat, Calgarian Kaillie Humphries and Heather Moyse of Toronto set a track record with a time of 53.19 seconds, then broke it with a second run of 53.01. They were an unstoppable force, but still saw room to improve. "My coach says I should try and drive the sled more like a Ferrari and less like a John Deere tractor," said Humphries, a first-time Olympian.

A MUTUAL FEELING?

In the middle of his team's 11-5 loss to China, American skip John Shuster stuck out his tongue and uttered for television viewers to hear, "I hate this stupid game." A teammate later said Shuster didn't mean it. The U.S. conceded early, cementing an awful Olympic showing: a 2-7 record and last-place finish.

NEXT TIME, JUST DENT THE TWINE!

Now that's a shot: defenceman Shea Weber scored Canada's second goal against Germany, beating netminder Thomas Greiss on his stick side, but no one knew it at first because the puck went right through the netting. "The net moved but the puck wasn't in it," Weber said. "It was kind of weird." A video review confirmed the goal.

Courage on ice

BY JAMES MCCARTEN

EVEN ON a day of gold medals and high-scoring Canadian hockey, the night belonged to Joannie Rochette.

Just days after the sudden death of her 55-year-old mother Thérèse, the diminutive 24-year-old skater from Île-Dupas, Que., was the picture of focus as she took to the ice to a thunderous ovation, then skated her heart out.

Rochette, the reigning world silver medallist and six-time Canadian champion, delivered a sultry tango to "La Cumparsita" that had the crowd clapping in time as if to will the skater along.

The result: a personal-best score, a shot at the podium and a nation inspired by an exceptional display of personal courage. "I think her mother gave her wings," said Nathalie Lambert, Canada's chef de mission.

When it was over, Rochette's strained figure-skater smile gave way to an outpouring of emotion. Hand over heart, she acknowledged the crowd, hugged her coach, then blew tearful kisses into the stands.

In comments relayed through a Skate Canada director, Rochette said words could not describe how she was feeling. "Hard to handle, but appreciate the support," she said of the ovation. "Will remember this forever."

It's a safe bet she wasn't alone.

Earlier in the day, Ashleigh McIvor of Whistler, B.C., embraced woolly whiteout conditions at Cypress Mountain, soaring into Olympic lore as the world's first gold medallist in the high-drama thrill ride that is women's ski cross.

On a course resembling a motocross track on the side of a mountain, four skiers bash elbows and catch massive air as they rip down a lane littered with huge jumps and turns. First over the line is the winner.

"I was pretty calm the whole way through, and just looking forward to each run," said the telegenic 26-year-old. "I was like, 'Let me go, let me go.'"

On the ice, Team Canada borrowed some of McIvor's momentum and dispatched middling Germany by a convincing 8-2 margin, a palate cleanser of a game that allowed a hockey-mad country to brace for the next day's clash with Alex Ovechkin and the Russians.

"It's going to be intense," Canadian star Sidney Crosby said of the faceoff against Russia, which eliminated Canada from the 2006 Games in Turin in the quarter-finals.

While Team Canada avoided disappointing a hockey-mad nation, world champion speedskater Sven Kramer, from the skating-crazy Netherlands, was not as lucky.

FREESTYLE SKIING   GOLD

Ashleigh McIvor poses with her ski-cross gold medal during the ceremony at B.C. Place. (Adrian Wyld/The Canadian Press)

Kramer, the world-record holder, was cruising to his second gold medal of the Games when his coach blundered and ordered him to stay in the inside lane instead of switching to the outside. Eight laps later, Kramer finished four seconds ahead of South Korea's Lee Seung-hoon — and was promptly disqualified. He threw his glasses away in disgust upon learning the news.

"With two or three laps to go, I was looking at my girlfriend in the stands and she had her face in her hands," he said later. "I thought, 'This is not good.'"

FREESTYLE SKIING GOLD

Ashleigh McIvor clears a jump ahead of France's Marion Josserand (right) and Hedda Berntsen of Norway during the women's ski-cross final. (Sean Kilpatrick/The Canadian Press)

FANS OF THE STONES

Japanese curling fans — one of whom
seemingly didn't get that text message about
which hat to wear — take in women's action
at the Vancouver Olympic Centre.

(Nathan Denette/The Canadian Press)

ALPINE SKIING

Patrick Biggs of Orleans, Ont., gets his head tangled in a gate during his first run of the men's giant slalom.

(Jacques Boissinot/The Canadian Press)

CANADIAN SYMBOLS (pages 138-139)

Members of the RCMP's Musical Ride pose in front of the Olympic cauldron.

(Adrian Wyld/The Canadian Press)

FIGURE SKATING

Canadian figure skater Joannie Rochette fights back tears following her short program in the women's competition.

(Paul Chiasson/The Canadian Press)

FIGURE SKATING

Cynthia Brossard of Contrecoeur, Que., responds to the crowd after her short program at the Pacific Coliseum. Brossard, 22, stood 15th. (Paul Chiasson/The Canadian Press)

BOBSLED

Like peas in a pod, Canada's four-man bobsled team — from left to right, Neville Wright, Jesse Lumsden, Justin Kripps and Pierre Lueders — race down the track during a training run. (Jeff McIntosh/The Canadian Press)

BIATHLON

Zina Kocher of Canmore, Alta., shoots in the women's four-by-six-kilometre relay in Whistler. The team of Kocher, Megan Imrie, Rosanna Crawford and Megan Tandy placed 15th. (Andrew Vaughan/The Canadian Press)

I SPY…

Skier Patrick Biggs peeks through one of his skis after completing a run during the men's giant slalom.

(Matthew McCarthy/The Canadian Press)

DAY 13

OUT OF GAS?

Canada's cross-country skiing men were crushed after a seventh-place finish in a relay in which they were touted as medal contenders. Devon Kershaw of Sudbury, Ont., seemed on fire earlier in the week in the team sprint, but fell apart after a promising first lap of the four-by-10-kilometre race. "I put the foot to the floor and nothing responded," he said.

DAMAGED DIGIT

In the women's giant slalom at Whistler, American skiing superstar Lindsey Vonn's run of bad luck continued as she crashed out of the race, bashing her knee into her chin and breaking a pinkie finger. "Things don't seem to be quite going my way," Vonn said.

WEIR'S RETORT TO RDS

American figure skater Johnny Weir was looking for understanding, not an apology, after broadcasters on French-language RDS said Weir hurt figure skating's image and should be subjected to a gender test. Weir called on the broadcasters to consider the impact their words would have on others, particularly impressionable youngsters. "I want them to think before they speak," he said.

Wicked Wednesday

BY JAMES MCCARTEN

ANATOMY OF a Canadian personal best: a one-two podium punch in bobsled, an unexpected speedskating silver and a third-place swan song from a bronze-haired flag-bearer.

This was the day the women went to work, giving Canada its best day of the Vancouver Games.

It began with Canadian long-track sweetheart Clara Hughes wearing the Maple Leaf flag like Superman's cape, jogging a victory lap and beaming at the crowd after earning a bronze medal in the women's 5,000 metres, the last race of her career.

It ended with Kaillie Humphries of Calgary and Heather Moyse of Summerside, P.E.I., basking in the joy of gold in the women's two-man bobsled, their teammates Helen Upperton of Calgary and Shelley-Ann Brown of Pickering, Ont., taking the silver behind them.

"I don't know how Canada feels, but if it's anything like I'm feeling, it's pretty exciting," said an elated Humphries.

Along with a surprise silver in the women's 3,000-metre short-track relay, it was a red-letter, four-medal day — the country's best one-day Winter Games total, matched by two Summer Games days in Turin, Italy, in 2006, and two in Salt Lake City in 2002.

And then, of course, there was The Game.

After all the hand-wringing and worry, a polished, poised men's hockey team advanced to the semifinals by summarily dispatching a Russian squad that ended up looking more like a teddy than a bear.

"We put out an effort as good as we've had in this tournament," forward Ryan Getzlaf said of the lopsided 7-3 win.

Russian goaltender Ilya Bryzgalov, who replaced Evgeni Nabokov to face the Canadian firing squad midway through the second period, described the pain the loss would cause in his home country.

"It's a disaster," Bryzgalov said. "End of the world."

The win had a particularly vengeful flavour for Team Canada, which was eliminated by Russia 2-0 in the quarter-finals in 2006 — a stinging loss that prompted a lot of soul-searching at home. It was also the first Canadian win over Russia in an Olympic matchup since 1960, when Team Canada beat what was then the Soviet Union at Squaw Valley, Calif.

For Hughes, from Glen Sutton, Que., the bronze was a thrilling end to a sparkling career that included five other Olympic medals, two of them as a cyclist in the Summer

WOMEN'S   RESULTS   HEAT 4
17 IRL-1 HOEY A.   3:38.84 +6.56
18 RUS-2 FEDOROVA   3:41.40 +9.12
19 AUS-1 LOCH-WI.
   GBR-1 MINICHI.   DNS
   GER-2 MARTIN.   DSQ

BOBSLED GOLD & SILVER

Canada's gold and silver medallists — from left, Kaillie Humphries, Helen Upperton, Heather Moyse and Shelley-Ann Brown — celebrate their one-two finish at the Whistler Sliding Centre.

(Mathew McCarthy/The Canadian Press)

Games. "That was one of the best races I've ever done," said Hughes.

In the women's 3,000-metre short-track relay, just moments before the hockey game ended, Canada's four-skater team of Jessica Gregg, Kalyna Roberge, Marianne St-Gelais and Tania Vicent finished third — but were promoted to silver after the first-place South Koreans were disqualified for a rules violation.

"We're always going for gold," said Vicent, 34, of Laval, Que., who was celebrating the fourth straight Olympics in which she has claimed a medal. "If you go for bronze, you might wind up fourth."

BOBSLED GOLD

Kaillie Humphries (left) and Heather Moyse embrace after winning the gold medal, a first for Canadian women bobsledders. The duo set track records on three of their four runs.

(Jeff McIntosh/The Canadian Press)

BOBSLED GOLD & SILVER

Canada's bobsledders wave the Maple Leaf after the flower ceremony. From left to right: Shelley-Ann Brown, Helen Upperton, Kaillie Humphries and Heather Moyse.

(Jeff McIntosh/The Canadian Press)

SHORT-TRACK SPEEDSKATING SILVER

The Canadian team — from left to right, Tania Vicent, Valérie Maltais (who did not skate), Marianne St-Gelais, Kalyna Roberge and Jessica Gregg — celebrate their silver medal in the women's 3,000-metre short-track relay.

(Robert Skinner/The Canadian Press)

SPEEDSKATING

Cindy Klassen skates for Canada in the women's 5,000-metre long-track race. She finished 12th, while teammate Kristina Groves placed sixth. (Adrian Wyld/The Canadian Press)

SPEEDSKATING   BRONZE

Clara Hughes lets out a whoop as she displays the bronze medal she won in the women's long-track 5,000 metres. In the final race of her career, Hughes set a track record of 6:55.73, a mark that was soon shattered by silver medallist Stephanie Beckert of Germany and gold medallist Martina Sablikova of the Czech Republic. (Darryl Dyck/The Canadian Press)

HOCKEY

Rick Nash (61) is congratulated by teammate Scott Niedermayer after scoring a goal in the first period of men's quarter-final action. Team Canada defeated the Russian squad, 7-3, to advance to the semifinals.

(Ryan Remiorz/The Canadian Press)

THE WEATHER

Workers tend the course after the first run of the women's giant slalom. Because of the fog that descended on Whistler Mountain, the second run was postponed. (Jacques Boissinot/The Canadian Press)

CROSS-COUNTRY SKIING

Canada's Alex Harvey races in the men's four-by-10-kilometre classic/free relay. The team of Harvey, Devon Kershaw, Ivan Babikov and George Grey finished seventh. (Boris Minkevich/The Canadian Press)

FIGURE SKATING

Joannie Rochette practises her routine for the free program. (Robert Skinner/The Canadian Press)

DAY 14

ROCK STARS

Kevin Martin, whose rink went a perfect 9-0 in round-robin competition, claimed a 6-3 victory over 24-year-old Niklas Edin of Sweden, putting Canada in the men's gold-medal game for the first time in eight years. Cheryl Bernard also earned a berth in the final by knocking off two-time silver medallist Mirjam Ott of Switzerland 6-5.

AERIAL MISHAPS

It was a chance for Canada's three aerialists to erase awful memories from Turin before an elated home crowd. But Kyle Nissen, Steve Omischl and Warren Shouldice each made critical errors that were difficult to swallow — especially for Nissen, who led after the first jump but struggled with his landing on his second attempt and finished fifth. Omischl was eighth, while Shouldice placed 10th.

REDEMPTION FOR ORSER

Twenty-two years after losing the Battle of the Brians in Calgary, Brian Orser finally hit Olympic gold — albeit vicariously, as Kim Yu-Na's coach. He said he felt enormous relief when Kim successfully landed a triple flip, the jump that cost him a gold. "I didn't want to have this ironic moment that she would not win the Olympic Games because of a bloody triple flip," he said.

Triumphs on ice

BY JAMES MCCARTEN

The heavy bronze medal around Joannie Rochette's neck seemed to lift some of the weight from her shoulders.

When her mother, Thérèse, suffered a fatal heart attack five days earlier, the lion-hearted figure skater knew she had no choice but to press on in the women's singles.

"That's what my mother would have wanted me to do," said the 24-year-old native of Île-Dupas, Que., who was the picture of determination as she twirled, floated and spun to an improbable podium finish. "That's how she raised me. She was always by my side. She was my biggest fan."

South Korean skating hero Kim Yu-Na, coached by former Canadian Olympic figure skater Brian Orser, easily won the gold, while Mao Asada of Japan took silver.

Rochette's bronze was Canada's first medal in women's singles since Elizabeth Manley won silver in Calgary in 1988.

Said John Furlong, the chief executive of Vancouver's Olympic organizing committee: "She was doing all the work, but my heart was going 200 beats a minute."

But it was clear that Rochette's Olympic joy would forever be tempered by tragedy.

"Tonight, she's happy," said Canadian chef de mission Nathalie Lambert. "But these Games will always be associated with something extremely sad. But at least with an ending that puts a little balm on the wound."

The skate put an exclamation mark on another triumphant day for Canada.

The host nation staked its claim in a pair of quintessentially Canadian sports with a gold-medal performance in women's hockey and semifinal victories in men's and women's curling that guaranteed both teams a shot at the top of the podium.

Marie-Philip Poulin of Beauceville, Que., scored twice and goaltender Shannon Szabados of Edmonton — a Games rookie — made 28 saves in a 2-0 win over the U.S., the first-ever shutout in an Olympic women's hockey final.

"This medal is Canada's medal," said centre Meghan Agosta of Ruthven, Ont., who was named the tournament's most valuable player. "To be able to win a gold medal on home soil is an honour. We're going to cherish the moment for the rest of our lives."

The players were unanimous in their praise of Szabados. "She's just a rock," said defenceman Colleen

HOCKEY GOLD

Canada's women's hockey team salutes a crowd of red-clad, flag-waving fans at after their 2-0 victory over Team USA in the gold-medal game. (Ryan Remiorz/The Canadian Press)

Sostorics, of Kennedy, Sask. "We played with confidence in front of her."

The win gave Canada its eighth gold of the Games, a new Winter Olympics benchmark.

Afterward, in a move that drew the ire of the International Olympic Committee, players celebrated the win with an impromptu party on the ice, drinking champagne and beer while still wearing their uniforms, medals draped around their necks.

HOCKEY GOLD (page 158-159)

Members of Team Canada join hands to celebrate their gold medal.

(Jonathan Hayward/The Canadian Press)

BOBSLED   GOLD & SILVER

Members of Canada's two women's bobsled teams (left to right: gold medallists Kaillie Humphries and Heather Moyse, and silver medallists Helen Upperton and Shelley-Ann Brown) greet the fans at a medal presentation ceremony the day after their victorious runs at the Whistler Sliding Centre.

(Mathew McCarthy/The Canadian Press)

FIGURE SKATING   BRONZE

Joannie Rochette brushes aside a tear after winning the bronze medal. (Robert Skinner/The Canadian Press)

HOCKEY GOLD

Members of the women's hockey team — Haley Irwin (21), Meaghan Mikkelson (12), Colleen Sostorics (5), Rebecca Johnston (6) and Becky Kellar (4) — take their celebration onto the ice at Canada Hockey Place after the final game. The International Olympic Committee took a dim view of the on-ice festivities, prompting Hockey Canada to issue an apology.

(Scott Gardner/The Canadian Press)

FREESTYLE SKIING

Kyle Nissen spins through the air during the men's aerials final at Cypress Mountain. Leading the field after his first jump, Nissen fell to fifth overall after earning the next-to-worst score on his second run.

(Sean Kilpatrick/The Canadian Press)

CROSS-COUNTRY SKIING

Perianne Jones (right) of Almonte, Ont., hands off to Chandra Crawford of Canmore, Alta., in the women's four-by-five-kilometre classic/free relay. (Frank Gunn/The Canadian Press)

FREESTYLE SKIING

Steve Omischl of Canada makes a rough landing during the men's aerials final. The 31-year-old finished eighth. Teammate Warren Shouldice, despite earning the highest score of the evening on his second jump, finished 10th. (Sean Kilpatrick/The Canadian Press)

CROSS-COUNTRY SKIING

Madeleine Williams of Edmonton competes in the final leg of the women's four-by-five-kilometre relay. The Canadian team finished 16th, nearly five minutes off the pace set by the gold medallists from Norway.

(Frank Gunn/The Canadian Press)

CROSS-COUNTRY SKIING

Daria Gaiazova of Banff, Alta., skis in the
women's four-by-five-kilometre relay.

(Frank Gunn/The Canadian Press)

CURLING

Canadian skip Cheryl Bernard blows a kiss to the crowd after defeating Switzerland 6-5 in a women's semifinal match.

(Nathan Denette/The Canadian Press)

CURLING

Swiss skip Mirjam Ott reacts after throwing her last rock of the semifinal match against Canada. Trailing 6-4 after nine ends, Ott made a last-ditch bid to tie the game, but scored only one point in the 10th end, giving Cheryl Bernard's rink the victory.

(Nathan Denette/The Canadian Press)

DAY 15

OLYMPIC DREAM OVER

Canadian cross-country ski coaches decided not to start Brian McKeever in the 50-kilometre mass-start classic race on the final day of the Games. McKeever, who is legally blind, was the first Canadian Paralympic athlete to be chosen for a Canadian Olympic team. "I have to be professional, and I have to choose those guys who are best for the 50-kilometre race," said coach Inge Braten.

AN IRANIAN FIRST

Marjan Kalhor made history in the women's slalom as the first Iranian to compete at the Winter Games. Wearing a pink hijab beneath her helmet, Kalhor came last among the 55 skiers who completed the race. But that didn't matter. "I'm proud," said Kalhor, 21. "We'll practise and practise, and we'll be better in the next Olympics."

NOT WATCHING THE CLOCK

The instant the Canadian women's pursuit team crossed the finish line in the quarter-finals, just five one-hundredths of a second behind the unheralded Americans, questions were raised about their decision not to be alerted to their opponents' lap times during the race. "Hindsight is 20/20," team member Kristina Groves said. "None of us had any clue that it was as tight as it was which is our own fault. We should have had maybe a better system."

The men mine for gold

BY JAMES McCARTEN

CHARLES HAMELIN became Canada's newest golden boy in more ways than one — two, to be exact.

The short-track speedskater from Ste-Julie, Que., claimed back-to-back trips to the top of the Olympic podium on Day 15, giving Canada a record-tying 10 gold medals and sole possession of the lead in Vancouver's first-place medal count.

"My goal was to bring back home one individual medal and one team medal," Hamelin said. "Two gold is the best I could have dreamed of."

With the victories, Canada not only added to its best-ever gold-medal haul at a Winter Games, but tied the record for the most ever awarded to a host country. The United States, in Salt Lake City in 2002, and Norway, in Lillehammer in 1994, both took 10 gold medals.

Hamelin, 25, made the most of his opportunities, first in a raucous 500-metre short-track final that also yielded a bronze for teammate François-Louis Tremblay — even though he never crossed the finish line — then again minutes later in a marathon four-man 5,000-metre relay.

Hamelin was joined in the 5,000 by his brother François, 23; Tremblay, 29, of Montreal; and Olivier Jean, 25, of Lachenaie, Que., as each took turns skating in an epic 45-lap battle.

"What we had hoped for was an exceptional day," said team leader and family patriarch Yves Hamelin. "To have results like that, all the planets have to be aligned. There are often unplanned things that happen in short-track. But today it was our turn and we had good races."

In the 500, Hamelin managed an ungainly first-place finish with U.S. superstar Apolo Ohno breathing down his neck — and Tremblay and Korea's Sung Si-Bak in a heap in the padding after crashing in the final turn. Ohno, however, was disqualified for a rules violation that triggered the crash, giving the silver to Sung and the bronze to Tremblay.

The men's hockey team eked out a 3-2 win over Slovakia — holding on to their tenuous lead during a mad six-man Slovakian scramble in the Canadian zone in the final minute — to advance to Sunday's gold-medal final against the U.S.

"It was two teams playing with a lot of desperation," said Canadian forward Brenden Morrow. "We wanted to get to the gold medal (game) and they wanted to just as bad. There were battles in there and bodies flying around, people paying the price."

Charles Hamelin kisses the gold medal he won after the men's 500-metre short-track final at the Pacific Coliseum.

(Paul Chiasson/The Canadian Press)

The hockey game and the short-track medals took the sting out of a stunning upset in women's long-track speedskating and a heartbreaking loss in the women's curling final.

Skip Cheryl Bernard lost a two-point lead over Sweden in the final end, then couldn't manage the double takeout needed to force another extra end. The notoriously boisterous Canadian crowd gasped and fell silent as the Swedes celebrated.

"Eventually, this silver's going to feel really great," said a teary-eyed Bernard, her voice breaking. "Just right now, the gold was very close."

SHORT-TRACK SPEEDSKATING   GOLD

Charles Hamelin rounds a turn, followed closely by Sung Si-bak of South Korea, in a 500-metre short-track quarter-final heat. Hamelin set an Olympic record in the race, with a time of 40.770 seconds.

(Paul Chiasson/The Canadian Press)

SHORT-TRACK SPEEDSKATING GOLD

(Left to right) Guillaume Bastille, François Hamelin, Charles Hamelin, Olivier Jean and François-Louis Tremblay stand atop the podium after the men's 5,000-metre relay.

(Paul Chiasson/The Canadian Press)

CURLING SILVER

Displaying mixed emotions, the members of Team Canada — from left to right, alternate Kristie Moore, lead Cori Bartel, second Carolyn Darbyshire, vice-skip Susan O'Connor and skip Cheryl Bernard — show off their silver medals after the women's curling final against Sweden.

(Nathan Denette/The Canadian Press)

SPEEDSKATING

(Left to right) Christine Nesbitt, Brittany Schussler and Kristina Groves race in the quarter-finals of the women's team pursuit. Canada lost the race to the U.S. by five one-hundredths of a second, ending their medal hopes. (Adrian Wyld/The Canadian Press)

CURLING

Eva Lund and Anna Le Moine of Sweden kiss
the winning rock after defeating Canada 7-6
in extra ends in the gold-medal draw. (Rick
Eglinton/The Canadian Press)

OH, WHAT A FEELING

Fans celebrate a Canadian goal during the first period of semifinal action against Slovakia. (Scott Gardner/The Canadian Press)

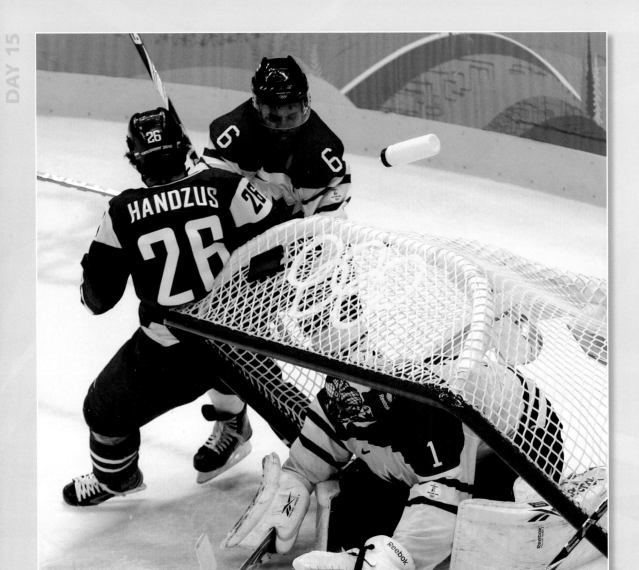

HOCKEY

Defenceman Shea Weber (6) checks Michal Handzus of Slovakia into the net, causing it to topple over and entrap goaltender Roberto Luongo. (Ryan Remiorz/The Canadian Press)

SNOWBOARD

Kimiko Zakreski of Calgary competes in a qualifying run for the women's parallel giant slalom. She lost an edge in her second run and did not advance to the quarter-final. Caroline Calvé of Aylmer, Que., also failed to qualify. Alexa Loo of Richmond, B.C., finished 12th.

(Darryl Dyck/The Canadian Press)

BOBSLED

The crew of Canada 2 — from left to right, Neville Wright, Jesse Lumsden, Justin Kripps and Pierre Lueders — race in the four-man competition. After two runs, the sledders were sixth, while Canada 1, piloted by Lyndon Rush, was in second. (Boris Minkevich/The Canadian Press)

ALPINE SKIING

Marie-Michèle Gagnon of Lac-Etchemin, Que., does a cartwheel in the finish area after her women's slalom run. Gagnon placed 31st. Top Canadian was Brigitte Acton of Sault Ste. Marie, Ont., in 17th, followed by Anna Goodman of Pointe-Claire, Que., in 19th and Erin Mielzynski of Guelph, Ont., in 20th.
(Mathew McCarthy/The Canadian Press)

GOT MITTS?

A young Canadian fan shows his support before the first run of the four-man bobsled competition. The red mittens were one of the most sought-after souvenirs of the Vancouver Games. (Jeff McIntosh/The Canadian Press)

SPEEDSKATING

Canadians Denny Morrison, Lucas Makowsky and Mathieu Giroux skate to an Olympic-record time of 3:42.38 in the quarter-final of the men's team pursuit at the Richmond Olympic Oval. They were even faster in the semifinal, posting a time of 3:42.22.
(Adrian Wyld/The Canadian Press)

DAY 16

NOTEWORTHY DEBUT

Ghana's first Winter Olympian, Kwame Nkrumah-Acheampong — known as the "Snow Leopard" — fulfilled his goal of competing in the Olympics, outracing one skier, Albania's Erjon Tola. "It's great," he said. "Daddy is not last on the list."

HERITAGE MOMENT

It was an iconic Canadian scene: one of the country's best-known actors, watching one of the country's best-loved sports, with a book by one of its most famous writers. Donald Sutherland, who appeared in the Games' opening ceremonies, was also on hand for many of the curling matches – and he brought along a copy of Alice Munro's *Runaway* for entertainment during lulls in the action.

SPEED TAPS

The men's pursuit team introduced a new technique: on straightaways, the second and third skaters gently nudged the pace-setter on the butt, helping the often-tired leader maintain his speed. Coach Marcel Lacroix worked on the concept for three years and only allowed the team to unveil it during the Games so other teams wouldn't have time to copy it. "That gold was because of the push," said coach Marcel Lacroix. "It was so effective it was stupid."

Worth waiting for

BY JAMES MCCARTEN

CALL IT a 24-karat day.

For the first time ever in a Winter Games, Canada won three golds in one day, raising the total to 13 — an all-time, all-season best that tied the record for the most top-tier podium finishes by any nation in a Winter Olympic Games.

Lucky No. 13 went to Edmonton curling skip Kevin Martin after a convincing 6-3 win over Norway, the country that had denied him gold eight years earlier in Salt Lake City.

"Finally," a beaming Martin said. "It took a long time, a lot of years. The hard work's worth it."

After an impromptu rendition of "O Canada" from the boisterous partisan crowd, Martin's final shot crashed into one of two Norwegian rocks hugging the eight-foot ring, sealing the victory and sending third John Morris leaping into the arms of lead Ben Hebert. Second Marc Kennedy scooted down the ice to embrace his skip, a man they call the Bear.

"We're so proud of the whole experience," Kennedy said. "It's a great day for Canada: three gold medals. Forever, no one can ever take it away from us."

Norwegian skip Thomas Ulsrud, wearing the diamond-spangled Loudmouth Golf trousers that had become the team's trademark, joked: "I thought we couldn't lose in these pants."

Martin's medal came on the heels of two rapid-fire wins: one in men's speedskating, and the other in the fog-shrouded men's snowboard parallel giant slalom, where Jasey Jay Anderson, 34, the blueberry farmer from Val-Morin, Que., came from behind against the world's top-ranked rider, Benjamin Karl of Austria, to capture a long-awaited Olympic medal.

Anderson was the defending world champion but had failed to make the podium in three Olympic appearances. A few years ago, he nearly hung up his board to spend more time with his family. But he decided to give it one last shot.

"I hope they will be able to remember the day that their father realized his dreams," Anderson said after showing off his medal to his young daughters, who braved the cold, relentless rain at Cypress Mountain. "I wanted to be an example to myself, to my kids, to people that supported me, yeah, that I wasn't a quitter. That even though there's challenges, they're meant to be overcome."

The men's speedskating pursuit team — Denny Morrison, 24, of Fort St. John, B.C., clad in a Team Canada jersey;

CURLING GOLD

Canada's men's curlers — from left to right, alternate Adam Enright, lead Ben Hebert, second Marc Kennedy, vice-skip John Morris and skip Kevin Martin — proceed down the ice after receiving their gold medals. The raucous crowds at the Vancouver Olympic Centre made one of the most lasting impressions of the 2010 Winter Games.

(Rick Eglinton/The Canadian Press)

Mathieu Giroux, 24, of Montreal; and Lucas Makowsky, 22, of Regina — looked elated as they skated a victory lap holding a Canadian flag.

There were smiles all around afterward, and one of the most notable came from Morrison. A week earlier, he had been in complete misery after poor performances in the 1,000 and 1,500. But he carried the load in pursuit by leading four of the eight laps, creating a draft that made it easier for the skaters who followed.

Another bronze medal was added to Canada's count when the Canada 1 bobsled, driven by Lyndon Rush of Humboldt, Sask., missed out on silver by just a hundredth of a second. "It's starting to become triumphant now," the disappointed 29-year-old said of his podium finish.

SNOWBOARD GOLD

Jasey Jay Anderson displays his gold medal after the men's parallel giant slalom at Cypress Mountain.

(Sean Kilpatrick/The Canadian Press)

SPEEDSKATING GOLD

Canadian speedskaters Denny Morrison (left), Lucas Makowsky and Mathieu Giroux (right), winners of gold in the men's pursuit, show that their synchronized podium-leaping technique could still use some refining.

(Robert Skinner/The Canadian Press)

BOBSLED BRONZE

The crew of Canada 1 (left to right: pilot Lyndon Rush, Chris Le Bihan, Dave Bissett and brakeman Lascelles Brown) show off their bronze medals after the final heat of the four-man competition.

(Boris Minkevich/The Canadian Press)

SNOWBOARD GOLD

Jasey Jay Anderson shows his gold medal to his daughters Jora (left) and Jy.

(Darryl Dyck/The Canadian Press)

SPEEDSKATING GOLD

Canadian speedskaters (left to right) Denny Morrison, Lucas Makowsky and Mathieu Giroux race for the gold medal in the men's team pursuit. They defeated the American team of Brian Hansen, Chad Hedrick and Jonathan Kuck by 0.21 of a second.

(Robert Skinner/The Canadian Press)

ALPINE SKIING

Julien Cousineau of Lachute, Que., celebrates after his men's slalom run. He finished eighth overall — the only Canadian to crack the top 10. Michael Janyk of Whistler, B.C., was 13th, while Trevor White of Calgary came in 31st.

(Mathew McCarthy/The Canadian Press)

FIGURE SKATING

Ice-dance gold medallists Tessa Virtue and Scott Moir (clad in a Team Canada hockey sweater) perform during the exhibition gala at the Pacific Coliseum.

(Paul Chiasson/The Canadian Press)

FIGURE SKATING

Patrick Chan of Toronto puts all his effort into a spin during the exhibition gala.

(Paul Chiasson/The Canadian Press)

DAY 17

CHEERS HEARD ROUND THE WORLD

Canadians around the world celebrated Canada's hockey win. In London, patrons of the city's only Canadian bar — The Maple Leaf — lined up nine hours before game time. In Kandahar, Afghanistan, hundreds of Canadian soldiers and civilians watched the game in the middle of the night alongside a group of Americans. "No one is sleeping on this base!" said Farhaan Ladhani.

FROSTY WAGER

U.S. President Barack Obama owed Prime Minister Stephen Harper a few cold ones after the hockey game. The two leaders had a friendly bet: if Team Canada came out on top, Obama had to pick up a case of Molson Canadian for the PM. Had it gone the other way, Harper would have had to send Obama a case of Pennyslvania-brewed Yuengling.

SO CLOSE

Canadian cross-country skier Devon Kershaw entered the stadium as part of the lead pack among the sport's superstars in the 50-kilometre mass-start race and lunged to a photo finish that ended with him in fifth. "One and a half seconds from gold ... I'm going to leave this Olympics really proud of what we accomplished, but also you never know if you get another chance," said an emotional Kershaw.

Our best Games ever

BY PATTI TASKO

HOLLYWOOD COULDN'T have come up with a better ending.

Canada capped its Golden Games with the medal that mattered, beating the United States 3-2 in an Olympic hockey overtime thriller that had the country holding its collective breath.

Sidney Crosby whipped a low shot between Ryan Miller's legs seven minutes, 40 seconds into overtime to decide the last medal of the Vancouver Olympics. Then the celebration began — across the country, in bars and living rooms, hockey rinks and streets.

"I dreamed of this moment," said the 22-year-old Crosby. "It's pretty incredible."

It was a remarkable comeback for Canada after a deflating tying goal by U.S. winger Zach Parise, who sent the game into overtime with 24.4 seconds left.

Gold medal No. 14 for Canada broke the record for the most top-of-podium finishes at a Winter Games, previously shared by the Soviet Union (1976) and Norway (2002).

Canada's seven silver and five bronze gave the country a total of 26, beating by two its previous Winter Games record set in Turin in 2006. The total fell short of the goal set by Canadian Olympic officials of winning the most medals overall, but with the hockey gold, no one was complaining.

The joyous mood of the Games' final day was a far cry from the first moments, which had been tragic and uncomfortable, beginning with the death of a Georgian luger on a track deemed by some as too fast and dangerous. Early teething pains — bad weather, criticism in the international press — also had a nation questioning whether the drive to "own the podium" was more than it could handle.

But then the sun came out — not just in the sky but in the form of the first gold medal won by a Canadian at a Canadian-hosted Games: men's mogulist Alexandre Bilodeau.

Jacques Rogge, president of the International Olympic Committee, recalled his "Canadian friends" complaining in 1976 at Montreal and at Calgary in 1988 that they didn't win a gold medal. With Bilodeau, "they got it. That was the defining moment for me."

The country was still enjoying the afterglow from the hockey game when the closing ceremonies began. Catriona le May Doan finally got the chance to light the Olympic cauldron that a malfunction denied her in the opening ceremonies.

Next, Canada's flag was carried into B.C. Place by figure skater Joannie Rochette, much admired for her courage for competing just days after her mother, Thérèse, died of a heart attack.

"Yes, it's been a tough week for me," said Rochette. "But I want to walk into that stadium as a celebration ... and a big smile on my face. I want to celebrate with my teammates."

AT EASE

Canadian troops watch the gold-medal hockey game between Canada and the U.S. at Kandahar Airfield's New Canada House in Afghanistan.

(Steve Rennie/The Canadian Press)

The Canadian contingent were dressed in Cowichan sweaters, and some, like curler Kevin Martin, wore their medals around their necks.

Actors William Shatner, Catherine O'Hara and Michael J. Fox delivered a three-part monologue that poked fun at Canadians' politeness and the country's vast expanse.

There were several winking references to national stereotypes, from marching Mounties in miniskirts to dancing canoes, table-top hockey players, lumberjacks, beavers and moose. Michael Bublé rode a giant Mountie hat while performing "The Maple Leaf Forever." A succession of Canadian performers — including Nickelback, Alanis Morissette and Avril Lavigne — hammered out their hits.

There were serious moments, too. Toronto-born rock legend Neil Young hushed the crowd with his song "Long May You Run" as the Olympic flame was extinguished.

The show's final note looked to the present and future, with Toronto's k-os performing his "Eye Know Something" while hip-hop dancers filled the arena, moving to the music.

As is custom, Rogge used his final speech to thank the host country for its hospitality and warmth. "May we all take that spirit home with us.

"These were excellent and very friendly Games!"

CROSS COUNTRY SKIING

Canada's Devon Kershaw (28) skis to a fifth-place finish during the 50-kilometre mass-start classic at Whistler Olympic Park. Kershaw finished 1.6 seconds behind gold medallist Petter Northug of Norway. Behind him is teammate Alex Harvey (22), who placed 32nd. (Jeff McIntosh/The Canadian Press)

HOCKEY GOLD

Canada's Sidney Crosby waves a Canadian flag after the men's hockey medal ceremony at Canada Hockey Place. (Matt Slocum/The Associated Press)

HOCKEY GOLD

Team Canada poses for a photo after winning the gold medal against the Americans. Defenceman Shea Weber and forward Jonathan Toews were named to the tournament all-star team. Toews also won the IIHF Directorate Award as best forward.

(Jonathan Hayward/The Canadian Press)

HOCKEY GOLD

Sidney Crosby tosses his gloves and stick aside as he celebrates his gold medal winning overtime goal.

(Paul Chiasson/The Canadian Press)

Athletes cross the floor of B.C. Place, winding their way around the Olympic cauldron.
(Robert Skinner/The Canadian Press)

Members of Team Canada make their way into B.C. Place for the closing ceremonies.
(Sean Kilpatrick/The Canadian Press)

(Pages 202-203)
Streamers and indoor fireworks add to the festive mood as Vancouver's Winter Games draw to a close. (Nathan Denette/The Canadian Press)

David Bissett, winner of a bronze medal in the four-man bobsled, poses for camera-wielding members of Team Canada alongside figure-skating bronze medallist Joannie Rochette. (Nathan Denette/The Canadian Press)

Medal Standings

Ranked in order of gold medals won. Countries with the same number of gold are sorted according to silver medals, then bronze.

Country	GOLD	SILVER	BRONZE	TOTAL
Canada	**14**	**7**	**5**	**26**
Germany	10	13	7	30
United States	9	15	13	37
Norway	9	8	6	23
South Korea	6	6	2	14
Switzerland	6	0	3	9
China	5	2	4	11
Sweden	5	2	4	11
Austria	4	6	6	16
Netherlands	4	1	3	8
Russia	3	5	7	15
France	2	3	6	11
Australia	2	1	0	3
Czech Republic	2	0	4	6
Poland	1	3	2	6
Italy	1	1	3	5
Belarus	1	1	1	3
Slovakia	1	1	1	3
United Kingdom	1	0	0	1
Japan	0	3	2	5
Croatia	0	2	1	3
Slovenia	0	2	1	3
Latvia	0	2	0	2
Finland	0	1	4	5
Estonia	0	1	0	1
Kazakhstan	0	1	0	1

Spotlight on Canada

DAY 1 FRIDAY, FEBRUARY 12

No medal events

DAY 2 SATURDAY, FEBRUARY 13

BIATHLON

WOMEN'S 7.5-KILOMETRE SPRINT
Megan Tandy, Prince George, B.C., 22:07.7, 46th
Zina Kocher, Red Deer, Alta., 22:35.8, 65th
Rosanna Crawford, Canmore, Alta., 23:04.6, 72nd
Megan Imrie, Falcon Lake, Man., 23:17.0, 76th

FREESTYLE SKIING

WOMEN'S MOGULS
Jennifer Heil, Spruce Grove, Alta., 25.69, SILVER
Chloé Dufour-Lapointe, Montreal, 23.87, 5th
Kristi Richards, Summerland, B.C., 4.36, 20th

SKI JUMPING

NORMAL-HILL INDIVIDUAL
Mackenzie Boyd-Clowes, Calgary, 44th in qualification round, did not advance
Trevor Morrice, Calgary, 46th in qualification round, did not advance
Stefan Read, Calgary, 47th in qualification round, did not advance
Eric Mitchell, Calgary, 49th in qualification round, did not advance

SHORT-TRACK SPEEDSKATING

MEN'S 1,500 METRES
Olivier Jean, Lachenaie, Que., 2:18.806, 4th
Charles Hamelin, Ste-Julie, Que., 2:18.243 (in "B" final), 7th
Guillaume Bastille, Rivière-du-Loup, Que., disqualified from heats

SPEEDSKATING

MEN'S 5,000 METRES
Lucas Makowsky, Regina, 6:28.71, 13th
Denny Morrison, Fort St. John, Alta., 6:33.77, 18th

DAY 3 SUNDAY, FEBRUARY 14

BIATHLON

MEN'S 10-KILOMETRE SPRINT
Jean-Philippe LeGuellec, Quebec, 24:57.6, 6th

FREESTYLE SKIING

MEN'S MOGULS
Alexandre Bilodeau, Rosemère, Que., 26.75, GOLD
Vincent Marquis, Quebec, 25.88, 4th
Pierre-Alexandre Rousseau, Drummondville, Que., 25.83, 5th
Maxime Gingras, St-Hippolyte, Que., 24.13, 11th

LUGE

MEN'S SINGLES
Samuel Edney, Calgary, 3:14.840, 7th
Jeff Christie, Calgary, 3:15.823, 14th
Ian Cockerline, Calgary, 3:16.243, 20th

NORDIC COMBINED

MEN'S INDIVIDUAL NORMAL-HILL/ 10-KILOMETRE CROSS-COUNTRY
Jason Myslicki, Thunder Bay, Ont, 45th

SPEEDSKATING

WOMEN'S 3,000 METRES
Kristina Groves, Ottawa, 4:04.84, BRONZE
Clara Hughes, Glen Sutton, Que., 4:06.01, 5th
Cindy Klassen, Winnipeg, 4:15.53, 14th

DAY 4 MONDAY, FEBRUARY 15

ALPINE SKIING

MEN'S DOWNHILL
Erik Guay, Mont-Tremblant, Que., 1:54.64, 5th
Manuel Osborne-Paradis, Invermere, B.C., 1:55.44, 17th
Jan Hudec, Calgary, 1:56.19, 25th
Robbie Dixon, Whistler, B.C., did not finish

CROSS-COUNTRY SKIING

MEN'S 15-KILOMETRE FREE
Ivan Babikov, Canmore, Alta., 34:30.0, 8th
Alex Harvey, St-Ferréol-les-Neiges, Que., 34:55.6, 21st
George Grey, Rossland, B.C., 35:13.0, 29th
Gordon Jewett, Canmore, Alta., 36:17.9, 52nd

WOMEN'S 10-KILOMETRE FREE
Madeleine Williams, Canmore, Alta., 27:43.6, 51st

FIGURE SKATING

PAIRS
Jessica Dubé, St-Cyrille-de-Wendover, Que., and Bryce Davison, Huntsville, Ont., 187.11, 6th
Anabelle Langlois, Hull, Que., and Cody Hay, Edmonton, 179.97, 9th

SNOWBOARD

Men's Snowboard Cross
Mike Robertson, Canmore, Alta., SILVER
Robert Fagan, Cranbrook, B.C., 5th
Drew Neilson, North Vancouver, B.C., 11th
François Boivin, Jonquière, Que., 12th

SPEEDSKATING

Men's 500 Metres
Jamie Gregg, Edmonton, 70.26, 8th
Jeremy Wotherspoon, Red Deer, Alta., 70.282, 9th
Mike Ireland, Mississauga, Ont., 70.63, 16th
Kyle Parrott, Minnedosa, Man., 71.344, 21st

DAY 5 TUESDAY, FEBRUARY 16

BIATHLON

Men's 12.5-Kilometre Pursuit
Jean-Philippe LeGuellec, Quebec, 34:51.9, 11th

Women's 10-Kilometre Pursuit
Megan Tandy, Prince George, B.C., 34:02.2, 36th

LUGE

Women's Singles
Regan Lauscher, Red Deer, Alta., 2:49.021, 15th
Alex Gough, Calgary, 2:49.391, 18th
Meaghan Simister, Calgary, 2:50.470, 25th

SNOWBOARD

Women's Snowboard Cross
Maëlle Ricker, West Vancouver, B.C., GOLD
Dominique Maltais, Petite-Rivière-St-François, Que., 20th

SPEEDSKATING

Women's 500 Metres
Christine Nesbitt, London, Ont., 77.57, 10th
Shannon Rempel, Winnipeg, 78.82, 27th
Anastasia Bucsis, Calgary, 79.755, 34th

DAY 6 WEDNESDAY, FEBRUARY 17

ALPINE SKIING

Women's Downhill
Britt Janyk, Whistler, B.C., 1:42.21, 6th
Emily Brydon, Fernie, B.C., 1:47.88, 16th
Shona Rubens, Canmore, Alta., 1:48.53, 21st
Georgia Simmerling, West Vancouver, B.C., did not start

CROSS-COUNTRY SKIING

Men's Individual Sprint Classic
Stefan Kuhn, Canmore, Alta., 15th
Devon Kershaw, Sudbury, Ont., 23rd
Drew Goldsack, Red Deer, Alta., 40th
Brent McMurtry, Calgary, Alta., 41st

Women's Individual Sprint Classic
Daria Gaiazova, Banff, Alta., 22nd
Chandra Crawford, Canmore, Alta., 26th
Sara Renner, Canmore, Alta., 34th
Perianne Jones, Almonte, Ont., 41st

LUGE

Men's Doubles
Chris Moffat, Calgary, and Mike Moffat, Calgary, 1:23.398, 7th
Justin Snith, Calgary, and Tristan Walker, Calgary, 1:24.220, 15th

SHORT-TRACK SPEEDSKATING

Women's 500 Metres
Marianne St-Gelais, St-Félicien, Que., 43.707, SILVER
Jessica Gregg, Edmonton, 44.204, 4th
Kalyna Roberge, St-Étienne-de-Lauzon, Que., 44.824 (in "B" final), 6th

SNOWBOARD

Men's Halfpipe
Justin Lamoureux, Ottawa, 7th
Brad Martin, Ancaster, Ont., 23rd
Jeff Batchelor, Oakville, Ont., 32nd

SPEEDSKATING

Men's 1,000 Metres
Denny Morrison, Fort St. John, Alta., 1:10.30, 13th
Jeremy Wotherspoon, Red Deer, Alta., 1:10.35, 14th
François-Olivier Roberge, St-Nicolas, Que., 1:10.75, 20th
Kyle Parrott, Minnedosa, Man., 1:10.89, 24th

DAY 7 THURSDAY, FEBRUARY 18

ALPINE SKIING

Women's Super Combined
Shona Rubens, Canmore, Alta., 2:12.58, 12th
Emily Brydon, Fernie, B.C., 2:12.76, 14th
Georgia Simmerling, West Vancouver, B.C., did not start

BIATHLON

Men's 20-Kilometre Individual
Jean-Philippe LeGuellec, Quebec, 50:47.1, 13th

Women's 15-Kilometre Individual
Megan Tandy, Prince George, B.C., 46:04.3, 50th
Megan Imrie, Falcon Lake, Man., 47:05.8, 62nd
Zina Kocher, Red Deer, Alta., 48:19.3, 72nd
Rosanna Crawford, Canmore, Alta., 49:22.1, 76th

FIGURE SKATING

Men
Patrick Chan, Toronto, 241.42, 5th
Vaughn Chipeur, Calgary, Alta., 170.92, 23rd

SNOWBOARD

Women's Halfpipe
Mercedes Nicoll, Whistler, B.C., 6th
Sarah Conrad, Dartmouth, N.S., 18th
Palmer Taylor, Collingwood, Ont., 26th

SPEEDSKATING

Women's 1,000 Metres
Christine Nesbitt, London, Ont., 1:16.56, GOLD
Kristina Groves, Ottawa, 1:16.78, 4th
Shannon Rempel, Winnipeg, 1:18.174, 21st
Brittany Schussler, Winnipeg, 1:18.31, 25th

DAY 8 FRIDAY, FEBRUARY 19

ALPINE SKIING

Men's Super-G
Erik Guay, Mont-Tremblant, Que., 1:30.68, 5th
Jan Hudec, Calgary, 1:32.09, 23rd
Robbie Dixon, Whistler, B.C., did not finish
Manuel Osborne-Paradis, Invermere, B.C., did not finish

CROSS-COUNTRY SKIING

Women's 15-Kilometre Pursuit
Sara Renner, Canmore, Alta., 41:37.9, 10th
Madeleine Williams, Canmore, Alta., 44:11.2, 41st
Daria Gaiazova, Banff, Alta., 44:35.9, 47th
Perianne Jones, Almonte, Ont., 45:48.7, 57th

SKELETON

Men's
Jon Montgomery, Russell, Man., 3:29.73, GOLD
Jeff Pain, Calgary, 3:31.86, 9th
Michael Douglas, Kleinburg, Ont., disqualified

Women's
Mellisa Hollingsworth, Eckville, Ont., 3:36.60, 5th
Amy Gough, Abbotsford, B.C., 3:37.01, 7th
Michelle Kelly, Grande Prairie, Alta., 3:40.79, 13th

DAY 9 SATURDAY, FEBRUARY 20

ALPINE SKIING

Women's Super-G
Britt Janyk, Whistler, B.C., 1:22.89, 17th
Georgia Simmerling, West Vancouver, B.C., 1:25.21, 27th
Emily Brydon, Fernie, B.C., did not finish
Shona Rubens, Canmore, Alta., did not finish

CROSS-COUNTRY SKIING

Men's 30-Kilometre Pursuit
Ivan Babikov, Canmore, Alta., 1:15:20.5, 5th
George Grey, Rossland, B.C., 1:15:32.0, 8th
Alex Harvey, St-Ferréol-les-Neiges, Que., 1:15:43.0, 9th
Devon Kershaw, Sudbury, Ont., 1:16:23.6, 16th

SHORT-TRACK SPEEDSKATING

MEN'S 1,000 METRES
Charles Hamelin, Ste-Julie, Que., 1.24.329, 4th
François Hamelin, Montreal, 1.25.206, 5th

WOMEN'S 1,500 METRES
Tania Vicent, Laval, Que., 2:23.035, 8th
Kalyna Roberge, St-Étienne-de-Lauzon, Que.,
    2:47.998 (in semifinal), 13th
Valérie Maltais, Montreal, 2:23.722
    (in semifinal), 14th

SKI JUMPING

LONG-HILL INDIVIDUAL
Stefan Read, Calgary, 71.6, 46th
Mackenzie Boyd-Clowes, Calgary, 45th in
    qualification round, did not advance
Trevor Morrice, Calgary, 49th in qualification
    round, did not advance
Eric Mitchell, Calgary, 51st in qualification
    round, did not advance

SPEEDSKATING

MEN'S 1,500 METRES
Denny Morrison, Fort St. John, Alta., 1:46.93,
    9th
Mathieu Giroux, Montreal, 1:47.62, 14th
Lucas Makowsky, Regina, 1:48.61, 19th
Kyle Parrott, Minnedosa, Man., 1:52.67, 37th

DAY 10 SUNDAY, FEBRUARY 21

ALPINE SKIING

MEN'S SUPER COMBINED
Ryan Semple, Ottawa, 2:48.26, 15th
Michael Janyk, Whistler, B.C., 2:50.77, 26th
Louis-Pierre Hélie, Berthierville, Que.,
    2:51.58, 30th
Tyler Nella, Burlington, Ont., 2:52.65, 32nd

BIATHLON

MEN'S 15-KILOMETRE MASS START
Jean-Philippe LeGuellec, Quebec, 39:18.5,
    30th

WOMEN'S 12.5-KILOMETRE MASS START
No Canadians entered

BOBSLED

TWO-MAN
Pierre Lueders, Edmonton, and Jesse
    Lumsden, Hamilton, Ont., 3:27.87, 5th
Lyndon Rush, Humboldt, Sask., and David
    Bissett, Edmonton, 3:30.46, 15th

FREESTYLE SKIING

MEN'S SKI CROSS
Christopher Del Bosco, Sudbury, Ont., 4th
Davey Barr, Vancouver, 6th
Stanley Hayer, Kimberley, B.C., 10th

SPEEDSKATING

WOMEN'S 1,500 METRES
Kristina Groves, Ottawa, 1:57.14, SILVER
Christine Nesbitt, London, Ont., 1:58.33, 6th
Cindy Klassen, Winnipeg, 2:00.67, 21st
Brittany Schussler, Winnipeg, 2:04.17, 35th

DAY 11 MONDAY, FEBRUARY 22

CROSS-COUNTRY SKIING

MEN'S TEAM SPRINT FREE
Devon Kershaw, Sudbury, Ont., and Alex
    Harvey, St-Ferréol-les-Neiges, Que.,
    19:07.3, 4th

WOMEN'S TEAM SPRINT FREE
Daria Gaiazova, Banff, Alta., and Sara
    Renner, Canmore, Alta., 18:51.8, 7th

FIGURE SKATING

ICE DANCE
Tessa Virtue, London, Ont., and Scott Moir,
    Ilderton, Ont., 221.57, GOLD
Vanessa Crone, Aurora, Ont., and Paul
    Poirier, Unionville, Ont., 164.60, 14th

SKI JUMPING

TEAM
Mackenzie Boyd-Clowes, Calgary, Trevor
    Morrice, Calgary, Eric Mitchell, Calgary,
    and Stefan Read, Calgary, 294.6, 12th

DAY 12 TUESDAY, FEBRUARY 23

ALPINE SKIING

MEN'S GIANT SLALOM
Erik Guay, Mont-Tremblant, Que., 2:39.63,
    16th
Robbie Dixon, Whistler, B.C., 2:40.98, 24th
Patrick Biggs, Orleans, Ont., 2:44.83, 35th
Brad Spence, Calgary, 2:46.24, 48th

BIATHLON

WOMEN'S 4-BY-6-KILOMETRE RELAY
Megan Imrie, Falcon Lake, Man.; Zina
    Kocher, Red Deer, Alta.; Rosanna
    Crawford, Canmore, Alta.; and Megan
    Tandy, Prince George, B.C., 1:14:25.5, 15th

FREESTYLE SKIING

WOMEN'S SKI CROSS
Ashleigh McIvor, Whistler, B.C., GOLD
Kelsey Serwa, Kelowna, B.C., 5th
Julia Murray, Whistler, B.C., 12th
Danielle Poleschuk, Calgary, 19th

NORDIC COMBINED

TEAM LONG-HILL/4-BY-5-KILOMETRE
    CROSS-COUNTRY
No Canadians entered

SPEEDSKATING

MEN'S 10,000 METRES
No Canadians entered

DAY 13 WEDNESDAY, FEBRUARY 24

BOBSLED

WOMEN'S
Kaillie Humphries, Calgary, and Heather
    Moyse, Summerside, P.E.I., 3:32.28, GOLD
Helen Upperton, Calgary, and Shelley-Ann
    Brown, Pickering, Ont., 3:33.13, SILVER

CROSS-COUNTRY SKIING

MEN'S 4-BY-10-KILOMETRE RELAY
    CLASSIC/FREE
Devon Kershaw, Sudbury, Ont.; Alex
    Harvey, St-Ferréol-les-Neiges, Que.; Ivan
    Babikov, Canmore, Alta.; and George Grey,
    Rossland, B.C., 1:47:03.2, 7th

FREESTYLE SKIING

WOMEN'S AERIALS
Veronika Bauer, Toronto, 160.46, 15th

SHORT-TRACK SPEEDSKATING

WOMEN'S 3,000-METRE RELAY
Jessica Gregg, Edmonton; Kalyna Roberge,
    St-Étienne-de-Lauzon, Que.; Marianne St-
    Gelais, St-Félicien, Que.; and Tania Vicent,
    Laval, Que.; 4:09.137, SILVER

SPEEDSKATING

WOMEN'S 5,000 METRES
Clara Hughes, Glen Sutton, Que., 6:55.73,
    BRONZE
Kristina Groves, Ottawa, 7:04.57, 6th
Cindy Klassen, Winnipeg, 7:22.09, 12th

DAY 14 THURSDAY, FEBRUARY 25

ALPINE SKIING

WOMEN'S GIANT SLALOM
Marie-Michèle Gagnon, Lac-Etchemin, Que.,
    2:28.89, 21st
Britt Janyk, Whistler, B.C., 2:29.79, 25th
Shona Rubens, Canmore, Alta., 2:30.25, 28th
Marie-Pier Préfontaine, St-Sauveur, Que.,
    2:30.51, 29th

CROSS-COUNTRY SKIING

WOMEN'S 4-BY-5-KILOMETRE CLASSIC/
    FREE
Daria Gaiazova, Banff, Alta., Perianne
    Jones, Almonte, Ont., Chandra Crawford,
    Canmore, Alta., and Madeleine Williams,
    Canmore, Alta., 1:00:05.0, 15th

FIGURE SKATING

WOMEN'S
Joannie Rochette, Île-Dupas, Que., 202.64,
    BRONZE
Cynthia Phaneuf, Contrecoeur, Que., 156.62,
    12th

FREESTYLE SKIING

Men's Aerials
Kyle Nissen, Calgary, 239.31, 5th
Steve Omischl, North Bay, Ont., 233.66, 8th
Warren Shouldice, Calgary, 223.30, 10th

HOCKEY

Women's Gold-Medal Game
Canada (Meghan Agosta, Ruthven, Ont.; Gillian Apps, Unionville, Ont.; Tessa Bonhomme, Sudbury, Ont.; Jennifer Botterill, Winnipeg; Jayna Hefford, Kingston, Ont.; Haley Irwin, Thunder Bay, Ont.; Rebecca Johnston, Sudbury, Ont.; Becky Kellar, Hagersville, Ont.; Gina Kingsbury, Rouyn-Noranda, Que.; Charline Labonte, Fabreville, Ont.; Carla MacLeod, Calgary; Meaghan Mikkelson, St. Albert, Alta.; Caroline Ouellette, Montreal; Cherie Piper, Toronto; Marie-Philip Poulin, Beauceville, Que.; Kim St-Pierre, Châteauguay, Que.; Colleen Sostorics, Kennedy, Sask.; Shannon Szabados, Edmonton; Sarah Vaillancourt, Sherbrooke, Que.; Catherine Ward, Montreal; Hayley Wickenheiser, Shaunavon, Sask.) defeated U.S.A., 2-0. GOLD

NORDIC COMBINED

Individual Long-Hill/10-Kilometre Cross-Country
Jason Myslicki, Thunder Bay, Ont., 44th

DAY 15 FRIDAY, FEBRUARY 26

ALPINE SKIING

Women's Slalom
Brigitte Acton, Sault Ste. Marie, Ont., 1:45.93, 17th
Anna Goodman, Pointe-Claire, Que., 1:46.04, 19th
Erin Mielzynski, Guelph, Ont., 1:46.09, 20th
Marie-Michèle Gagnon, Lac-Etchemin, Que., 1:49.51, 31st

BIATHLON

Men's 4-by-7.5-Kilometre Relay
Robin Clegg, Ottawa; Marc-André Bédard, Valcartier, Que.; Brendan Green, Hay River, N.W.T.; and Jean-Philippe LeGuellec, Quebec, 1:24:50.7, 10th

CURLING

Women's Gold-Medal Game
Canada (Cheryl Bernard, Calgary; Susan O'Connor, Calgary; Carolyn Darbyshire, Calgary; Cori Bartel, Lanigan, Sask.; Kristie Moore, Grande Prairie, Alta.) were defeated by Sweden 7-6. SILVER

SHORT-TRACK SPEEDSKATING

Men's 500 Metres
Charles Hamelin, Ste-Julie, Que., 40.981, GOLD
François-Louis Tremblay, Montreal, 46.366, BRONZE
Olivier Jean, Lachenaie, Que., 9th, disqualified in semifinals

Men's 5,000-Metre Relay
Charles Hamelin, Ste-Julie, Que.; François Hamelin, Montreal, Que.; Olivier Jean, Lachenaie; and François-Louis Tremblay, Montreal, 6:44.224, GOLD

Women's 1,000 Metres
Kalyna Roberge, St-Étienne-de-Lauzon, Que., 1:32.122 (in "B" final), 5th
Jessica Gregg, Edmonton, 1:32.333 (in "B" final), 6th
Tania Vicent, Laval, Que., 17th, disqualified in quarter-finals

SNOWBOARD

Women's Parallel Giant Slalom
Alexa Loo, Richmond, B.C., 12th
Caroline Calvé, Aylmer, Que., 20th
Kimiko Zakreski, Calgary, 29th

DAY 16 SATURDAY, FEBRUARY 27

ALPINE SKIING

Men's Slalom
Julien Cousineau, Lachute, Que., 1:40.66, 8th
Michael Janyk, Whistler, B.C., 1:41.09, 13th
Trevor White, Calgary, 1:47.17, 31st

BOBSLED

Four-Man
Lyndon Rush, Humboldt, Sask.; David Bissett, Edmonton; Lascelles Brown, Calgary; and Chris Le Bihan, Kelowna, B.C., 3:24.85, BRONZE
Pierre Lueders, Edmonton; Justin Kripps, Summerland, B.C.; Neville Wright, Edmonton; and Jesse Lumsden, Hamilton, Ont., 3:25.60, 5th

CROSS-COUNTRY SKIING

Women's 30-Kilometre Mass-Start Classic
Sara Renner, Canmore, Alta., 1:34:04.2, 16th
Madeleine Williams, Canmore, Alta., 1:42:33.7, 46th

CURLING

Men's Gold-Medal Game
Canada (Kevin Martin, Edmonton; John Morris, Ottawa; Marc Kennedy, Edmonton; Ben Hebert, Regina; and Adam Enright, Edmonton) defeated Norway 6-3. GOLD

SNOWBOARD

Men's Parallel Giant Slalom
Jasey Jay Anderson, Val-Morin, Que., GOLD
Matthew Morison, Burketon, Ont., 11th
Michael Lambert, Toronto, 12th

SPEEDSKATING

Men's Team Pursuit
Mathieu Giroux, Montreal; Lucas Makowsky, Regina; and Denny Morrison, Fort St. John, Alta., 3:41.37, GOLD

Women's Team Pursuit
Kristina Groves, Ottawa; Christine Nesbitt, London, Ont.; and Brittany Schussler, Winnipeg, 3:01.41 (in "C" final), 5th

DAY 17 SUNDAY, FEBRUARY 28

CROSS-COUNTRY SKIING

Men's 50-Kilometre Mass-Start Classic
Devon Kershaw, Sudbury, Ont., 2:03:37.1, 5th
George Grey, Rossland, B.C., 2:06:18.1, 18th
Alex Harvey, St-Ferréol-les-Neiges, Que., 2:10:49.9, 32nd
Ivan Babikov, Canmore, Alta., 2:10:50.2, 33rd

HOCKEY

Men's Gold-Medal Game
Canada (Patrice Bergeron, Sillery, Que.; Dan Boyle, Ottawa; Martin Brodeur, Montreal; Sidney Crosby, Cole Harbour, N.S.; Drew Doughty, London, Ont.; Marc-André Fleury, Sorel, Que.; Ryan Getzlaf, Regina; Dany Heatley, Calgary; Jarome Iginla, St. Albert, Alta.; Duncan Keith, Penticton, B.C.; Roberto Luongo, Montreal; Patrick Marleau, Aneroid, Sask.; Brenden Morrow, Carlyle, Sask.; Rick Nash, Brampton, Ont.; Scott Niedermayer, Cranbrook, B.C.; Corey Perry, Peterborough, Ont.; Chris Pronger, Dryden, Ont.; Mike Richards, Kenora, Ont.; Brent Seabrook, Tsawwassen, B.C.; Eric Staal, Thunder Bay, Ont.; Joe Thornton, St. Thomas, Ont.; Jonathan Toews, Winnipeg; and Shea Weber, Sicamous, B.C.) defeated U.S.A. 3-2 in overtime. GOLD